Atlas of Pennsylvanian (Carboniferous) Age Plant Fossils of the Central Appalachian Coalfields

VOLUME 2

Thomas F. Mcloughlin
GEOLOGIST, M.S.

**ATLAS OF PENNSYLVANIAN (CARBONIFEROUS)
AGE PLANT FOSSILS OF THE CENTRAL APPALACHIAN
COALFIELDS – VOLUME 2**

Copyright © 2024 Thomas F. Mcloughlin

Because of the dynamic nature of the Internet, any web addresses or links contained in this book may have changed since publication and may no longer be valid. The views expressed in this work are solely those of the author and do not necessarily reflect the views of the publisher, and the publisher hereby disclaims any responsibility for them.

Library of Congress Control Number: 2023952585
Paperback: 979-8-89306-008-9
eBook: 979-8-89306-009-6

Printed in the United States of America

Contents

Pennsylvanian coal swamp vegetation reconstruction, a composite of many plant types growing in and around the swamp. An original drawing composed by John Hughes at http://www.jfhdigital.com/.

ACKNOWLEDGEMENT

This book could not have been completed without the ded-icated help of Dr. Shusheng Hu, who is a paleobotonist and Collections Manager Division of Paleobotony at the Yale Peabody Museum of Natural History in New Haven, Connecticut and Dr. Christopher Cleal, who is a paleobotanist with the museum in Wales in the UK. I also thank Dr. Bill Di Michele, Department of Paleobiology at the Smithsonian Institution National Museum of Natural History, for his review of the manuscript and helping with some of the fossil identifications. Dr. Jack Wittry, who is associ-ated with the Science and Education division of The Field Museum Chicago Illinois lent his assistance in fossil identification.

I also want to thank my wife, Beth, for her patience and tol-erance for the numerous boxes of fossil specimens in our home. She was very relieved when I donated the collection to the Virginia Museum of Natural History and the Peabody Museum in New Haven Connecticut.

All of the fossils listed in the plates were collected by and photo-graphed by the author except as noted.

FOREWORD

I have spent the last thirty-six years in and around the bituminous coal mines of southwestern Virginia, Kentucky and West Virginia. When coal miners learn I am a geologist, the most popular question has been "what are the kinds of fossils we see in a mine roof?" I give my best reply, but it is difficult to relate to them that the plant impressions represent vegetation that grew in peat-form-ing swamps millions of years ago. Most people recognize the fern-like fossils, but have been confused about the identity of a portion of tree root versus the tree itself. Many believe that the fossils are not those of ancient vegetation, but instead are the preserved remains of reptiles.

INTRODUCTION

In this Volume is presented another variety of plant fossils, many of which were donated by other collectors (mostly coal miners). This is because the availability of outcrops (road cuts) suit-able for collecting are becoming fewer and harder to find in the region. The best specimens are found in the mines. In addition to Virginia many fossils were found in Kentucky and West Virginia. Comparisons are made visually between some of the ancient plants and modern look- a-likes.

I became interested in geology because of the fossils and it is the goal of this publication is a pictorial guide to the identification of the more common Carboniferous age plant fossils from the coal fields. Those especially targeted are the rock hounds and aspiring geologists of all ages (Figure 1).

Figure 1. This reminds me so much of me that I have to share it with you.

To put in perspective the range of sizes of the trees that contrib-ute the largest proportion of plant fossils that were found during the development of this book and the previously published McLoughlin, T.F., 2017, two (2) tree charts are presented (See Figures 2 and 3) below. They are based on tree/plant heights listed in Kendrick,P and Paul Davis,2004, Cleal, C.J. and Barry A. Thomas, 1994, and Cross, A. T., et. al.,1996. It is to be noted that the *Cordaites* was among a group of plants that ranged widely in size from shrub-like to enormous. The variety of *Cordaites* that had mangrove-like root systems did not grow very large and no estimated growth size could be found in the literature as of the writing of this book. Therefore, the drawing of the mangrove-like *Cordaites* is show as one might envision a "shrub" tree or plant.

A relative to Lepidodendron and *Lepidophloios* and having char-acteristics intermediate between those of the fossil genera *Lepidodendron* and *Sigillaria, is Bothrodendron*. Like its relatives it was a *lycopod* related to modern club mosses. The Bothrodendron twigs classification is based upon seldom-forked branches with small leaves as compared to *Lepidodendron*. They grew up to 130 feet in height and about 7 feet in diameter.

No reconstruction of *Bothrodendron* could be found in the pres-ent day literature and therefore not shown in the tree chart.

Not all of the known variety of plants found in the Carboniferous coal fields of the world are shown, just those that were encoun-tered during collecting in Virginia, Kentucky and West Virginia (See Figure 11). In simplifying the sequence of steps described in McLoughlin, T.F., 2017 for the development of "kettlebottoms" and fossil standing tree trunks, and the danger present to under-ground coal miners by kettlebottomsis shown in a sketch taken from the Kentucky Geologic Survey's (KGS) websites are presented below (Figure 4). Also, from the KGS website (left) and a photo I took in the Pochanontas mine at Pochahontas, West Virginia (right) are kettlebottom in mine roof are shown in figure 5. To give an example, not a typical, Carboniferous forest scene illustrating the distribution of plants and trees based on soil conditions the sketch showing a section across a typical coal measures peat swamp was first presented by DiMichele and Phillips, 1994, then redrawn by others is included here as figure 6.

The various ages of the coal bed horizons from which fossils were collected in the Tri-State region are listed in a diagram of the modern Geologic Time Scale (Figure 7) and geologic stratigraphic columns in figures 8, 9 and 10. Counties from which the fossils were collected are shown in the index map of the region (Figure 11).

Beware of the inorganic objects that look like fossil plants or animals. These are the look-a-likes that are not ferns, snakes or fish. The most common mineral residue left by water that traveled along cracks in the rocks are dendrites. These closely resemble the fern group *Sphenopteris*. A variation on pseudofossil is an impression of a tree limb or bark and appears to be scales of reptile skin. I was very skeptical of the stories told by coal miners that they had found a snake or a fish because they had no physical or photographic evi-dence. The "fossill" would disintegrate or fall apart as the miner tried to extract it from the mine roof. I finally found a form in a rock in the roof of a coal mine that was said to be a fish and I now had a photograph representing at least one form that looks like a fish. It turns out that it is a fossil fish. I believe the impression of the *Lepiodendron* and *Lepidophloios* stems and branches would look like a snake skin because the fossil shows "scale-like" patterns and often a sinuous shape. Gillespie,1978, also includes waterworn pebbles that resemble seeds, which even can fool the experienced collector and specialist. Forms that are often referred to as "Kettlebottoms" in the eastern coal fields because they fall from the mine roof or are excavated in strip mines leave a nearly circular cavity are actually concretions. Trace fossils are the tracks or trails left in the sediment that, when it turned to rock, left markings that could be mistaken for the living creature itself, such as worm trails (See plate I).

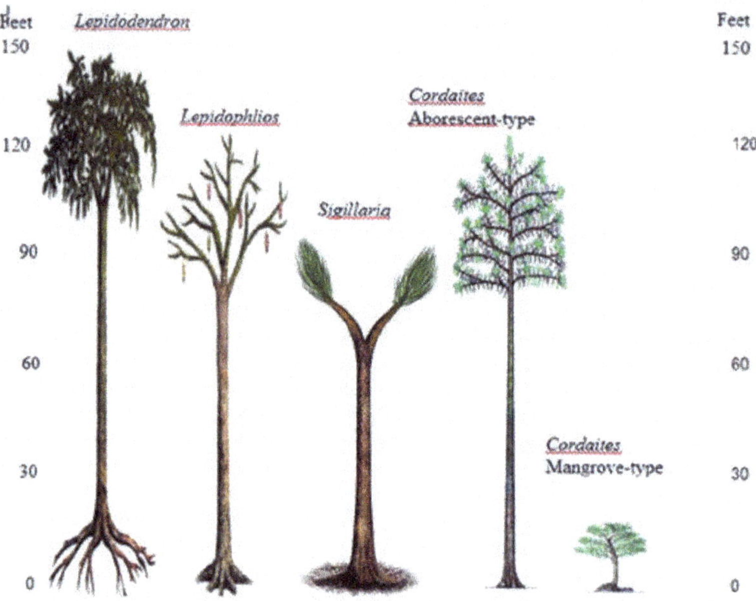

Figure 2: *Shown are the various types (genera) of lycopod and early conifers trees from Pennsylvanian-age coal fields. The trees are drawn at their estimated growth height, except for Cordaites mangrove-type. It is shown as a "shrub" sized plant. Heights of trees are based mostly on downed logs preserved as fossils. There are standing fossil tree stumps ("kettlebottoms") and large portions of the upright tree trunk itself, which also include calamities and fern trees. The trees shown are a compi-lation of the sources of the fossils displayed in this publication.*

Figure 3: *The trees shown are at their estimated growth height and are sources of the fossils displayed in this publication. The lycopod trees Diaphorodendron and Bothrodendron were taken from the webpage http://www.uky.edu/KGS/fossils/ fossil-tree-stumps-types.php (the Kentucky Geologic Servey).*

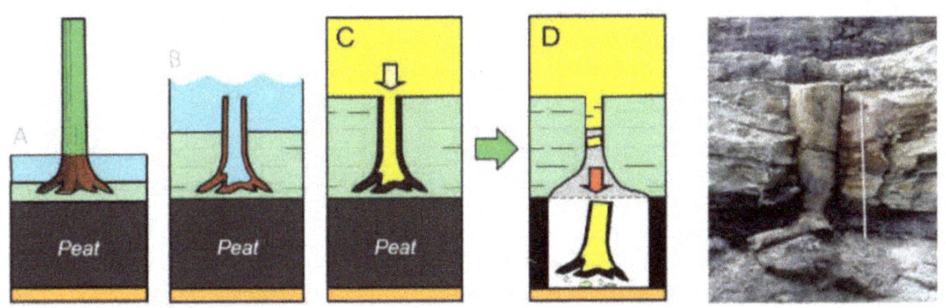

Figure 4: *Here is the general sequence of the development of "kettlebottoms" and standing tree trunks. (A) Living tree. Death, hollowing, and rapid burial. (C) Infilling of hollowed-out, tree-forming an internal cast and mold. (D)*

The external cast and/or mold of the fossil tree stump can fall out of mine roof. Also, see McLoughlin, T.F., 2017. This illustration presented by permission of Steve Greb with the Kentucky Geological Survey (KGS) and taken from the KGS web site page at http://www. uky.edu/KGS/ coal/coal-mining-geology-Kettlebottoms. php and http:// www.uky.edu/KGS/fossils/fossil-tree-stumps-form.php.

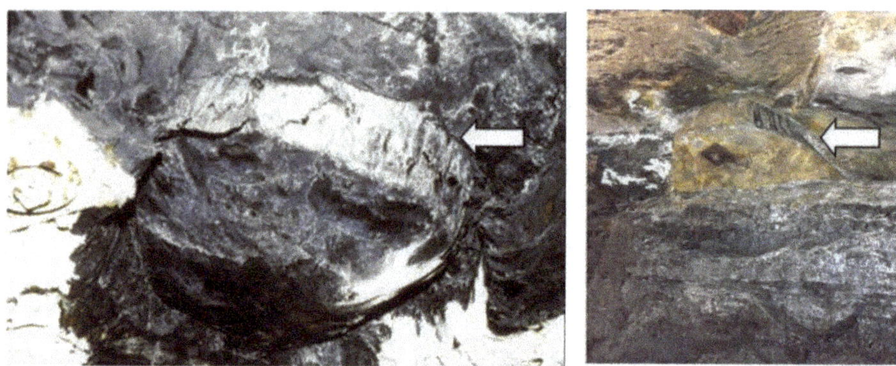

Figure 5: *Pictures of kettlebottoms (arrows) in underground coal mine roof. The one on the left is preserved in shale (See KGS web site page in figure 4) and in sandstone on the right.*

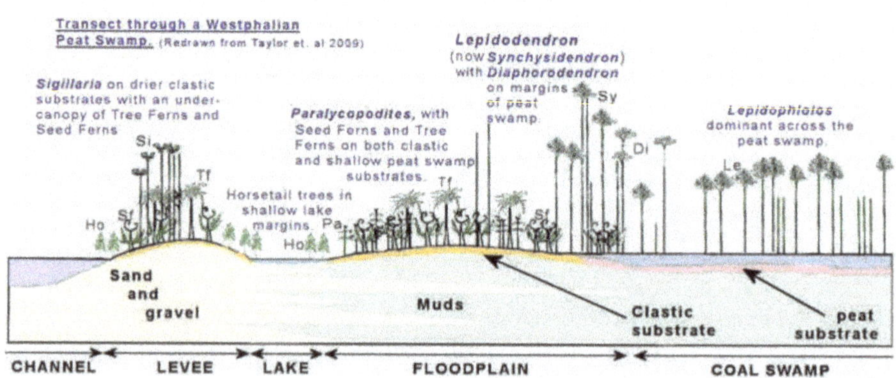

Figure 6: *Sketch Section across a typical coal measures peat swamp. Redrawn from Taylor et al., 2009 by Sheffield Area Geology Trust, for the article The Palaeoecology of Aborescent Lycopods, posted on the internet at http://www. geologyatsheffield.co.uk/sagt/palaeoecology/. The diagram was originally derived from DiMichele and Phillips, 1994.*

Plate I 1. Dendrites (Courtesy of the West Virginia Geological and Economic Survey). 2. Lepidophloios ("scale bark") stem Leslie County, Kentucky. 3 Lepidodendron ("scale tree") Grundy, Buchanan County, Virginia 4. Concretion, Pound, Wise County, Virginia (looks like a "kettlebot-tom" or tortes shell) 5. Fossil fish in the Pocahontas museum mine in Pocahontas, West Virginia. 6. Worm trails (dark graylines) from Cave Run Lake area near Morehead, Kentucky. 7,7a Weathered limestone concer-tation (looks like a horse's hoof).

PLATE I

Geologic Time Scale*

Era	Period		Epoch	
Cenozoic	Quaternary		Holocene (Recent)	0.01 myrs***
			Pleistocene	
	Tertiary	Neogene	Pliocene	
			Miocene	
				23 myrs
		Paleogene	Oligocene	
			Eocene	
			Paleocene	
				66 myrs
Mesozoic (Middle Life)	Cretaceous			
	Jurassic			
	Triassic			
				252 myrs
Paleozoic	Permian			299 myrs
	Carboniferous	Pennsylvanian (Upper)		307 myrs
		Pennsylvanian (Middle)		315 myrs
		Pennsylvanian (Lower)		323 myrs
		Mississippian		
	Devonian			359 myrs
	Silurian			
	Ordovician			
	Cambrian			
				541 myrs
Precambrian				4,000 myrs

* Modified from Geologic Time Scale posted on the United States Geological Survey Web site.

** Millions of Years Before Present

Figure 7: *General geologic time scale showing the ages of peat formation during the Carboniferous (Pennsylvanian). Refer to figures 8 through 10 for the actual chronologic sequence the coal beds from which plant fossils were collected.*

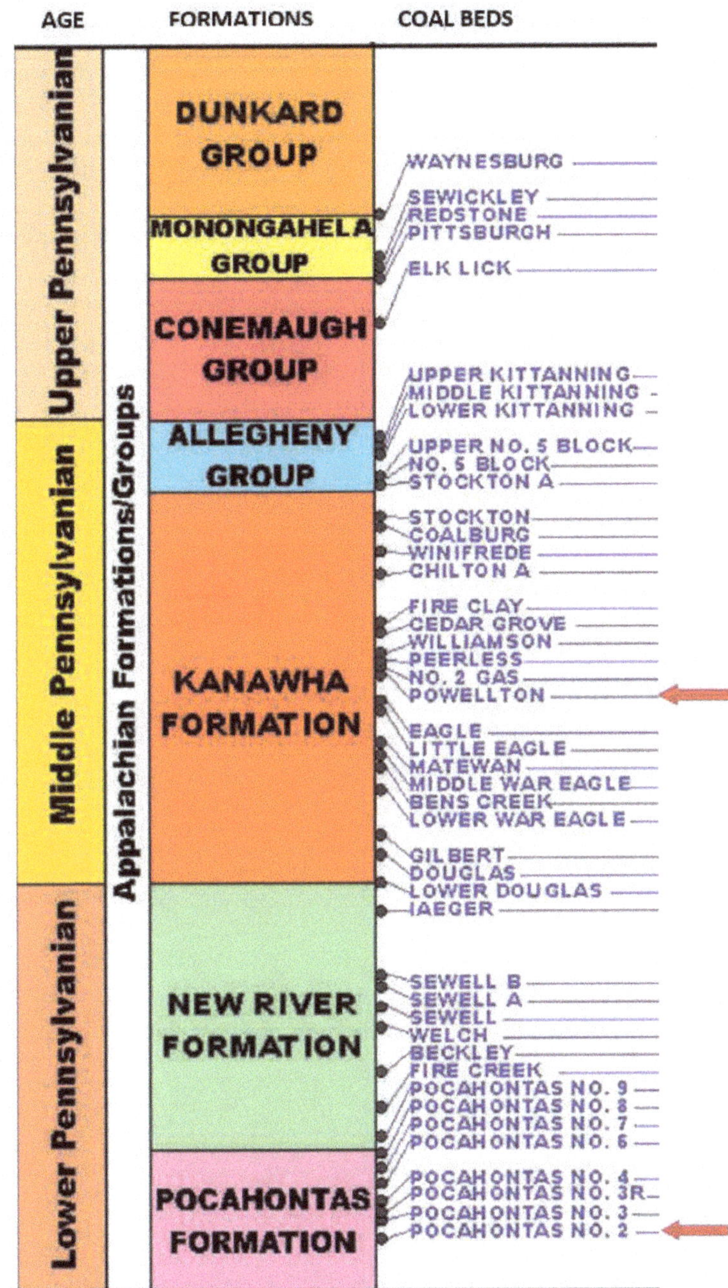

Figure 8: Geologic column of the mineable coal beds in West Virginia. The red arrows point to the coal beds where fossils were collected for this book. Modified from the West Virginia Geological and Economic Survey, 2001.

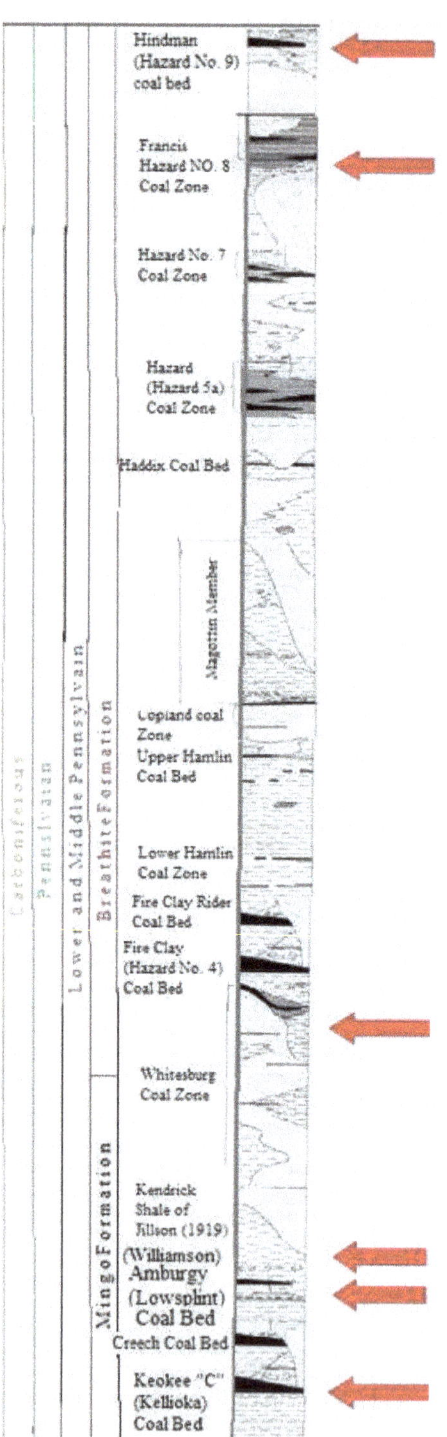

Figure 9: Geologic column of the mineable coal beds in the Eastern Kentucky Coal Field. The red arrows point to the coal beds where fossils were collected for this book. The information was compiled from the Vicco geologic map by Willard D. Puffett, 1965, Hyden West geologic map by Richard Q. Lewis, Sr., 1978 and Robert C. McDowell, 2001.

			Geologic Formation	Coal bed/coal zone
Carboniferous	Pennsylvanian	Upper Pennsylvanian	Harlan	Unnamed (No. 14) No. 13
			Wise	High Splint Morris Pardee (Parsons) ← Wax Gin Creek (No. 8) Phillips (Wallins) ← Jack Rock Little Red House Low Splint (Creech) 34-Inch (Cedar Grove) Owl Taggart (Darby) ← Taggart Marker (Kellioka) ← Wilson (Alma, Harlan, Upper Standiford) Upper St. Charles (Redwine, Standiford) Pinhook Kelly (Upper Bolling) Imboden (Campbell Creek, Lower Bolling, Pond Creek) ← Clintwood ← Blair ← Lyons (Eagle) Dorchester ←
			Norton / upper Norton	Norton ← Hagy (Edwards) Splash Dam ← Upper Banner Middle Banner **Lower Banner** ← Kennedy ←
		Lower Pennsylvanian	Lee / lower Norton	Aily Raven (Red Ash) Jawbone Tiller Greasy Creek Lower Seaboard Bandy Upper Horsepen
			Pocahontas	Pocahontas No. 5 Pocahontas No. 3 ← Pocahontas No. 2 Pocahontas No. 1 Pocahontas (stratigraphic position uncertain) Other

Figure 10: *Geologic column of the mineable coal beds in the Southwestern Virginia Coal Field. The red arrows point to the coal beds where fossils were collected for this book. The chart is modified after the Virginia Division of Geology and Mineral Resources, 2015.*

Figure 11: *Index map to the study area where fossil flora have been collected from southwestern Virginia, southeastern Kentucky and southwestern West Virginia.*

CHAPTER 1

ABORESCENT LYCOPODS (CLUB MOSSES, SCALE TREES)

LEPIDODENDRON

LEPIDODENDRON –This plant is sometimes referred to as a "scale tree" because of the distinctive tear drop or diamond shape pattern of the bark. It is often mistaken as the scales of a reptile or snake's skin. Each scale-like feature is accented by a small depression that looks like an eye. These plants where common during the Carboniferous (See Figure 12).

Figure 12. Drawing of Lepidodendrons courtesy of Jon Hughes/www. jfhdigital. com.

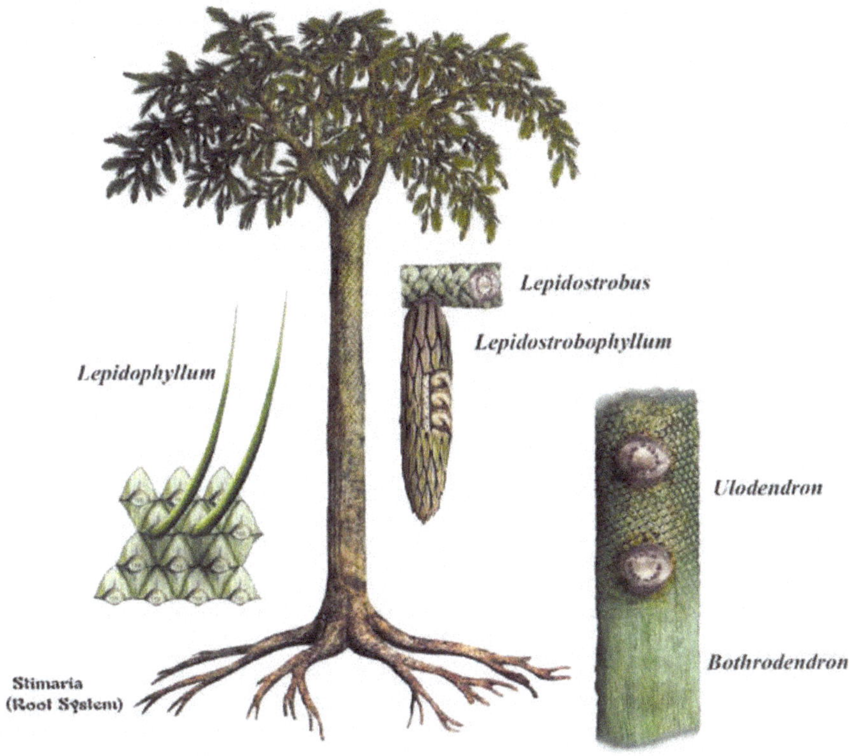

Figure 13: *Basic elements of Lepidodendron. Ulodendron and Bothrodendron are shown also. Compiled from graphics by Jon Hughes/ www.jfhdigital.com (tree) and by Langford, G., 1958, figure 100, page 64 by permission of Esconi Associates, Illinois.*

Before the anatomy of *Lepidodendron* (i.e. microscopic examination of the tissue cells) was understood, generic names for the plant stems were based on the various appearances of the same plant form resulting from preservation at different stages of decortica-tions, or states of decay. The generic terms for the wood layers which included *Knorria* and *Aspidiaria* have been retained for descriptive purposes only. These forms of stem casts are more fully discussed by Seward, (1898). The wood layers are illustrated in figure 14.

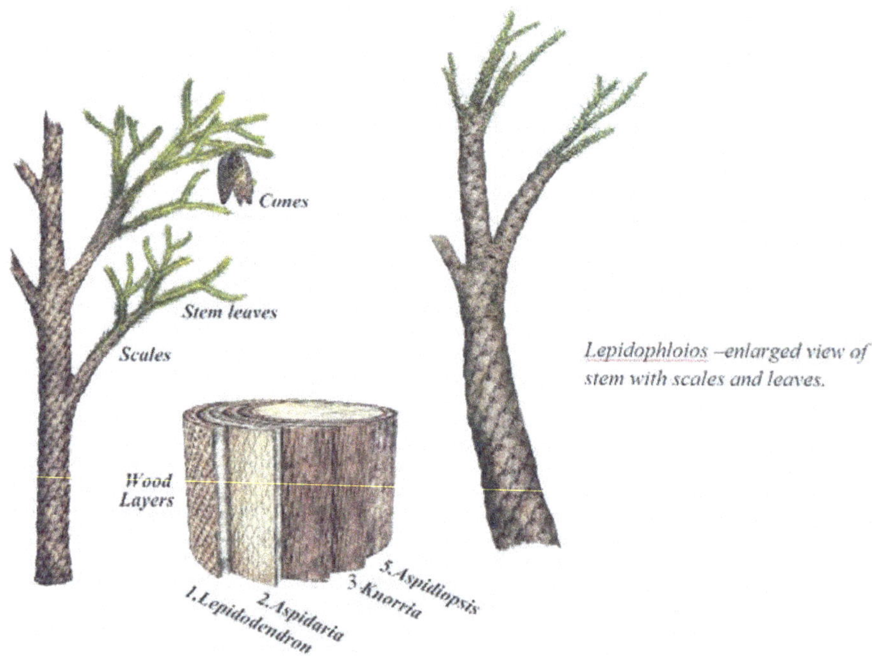

Figure 14: *Reconstruction of Lepidodendron showing wood layers and portions of the Lepidodendron and Lepidphloios tree often found as fossils. Drawings modified after Dinoera. com and colorized by Jon Hughes/www. jfhdigital.com.*

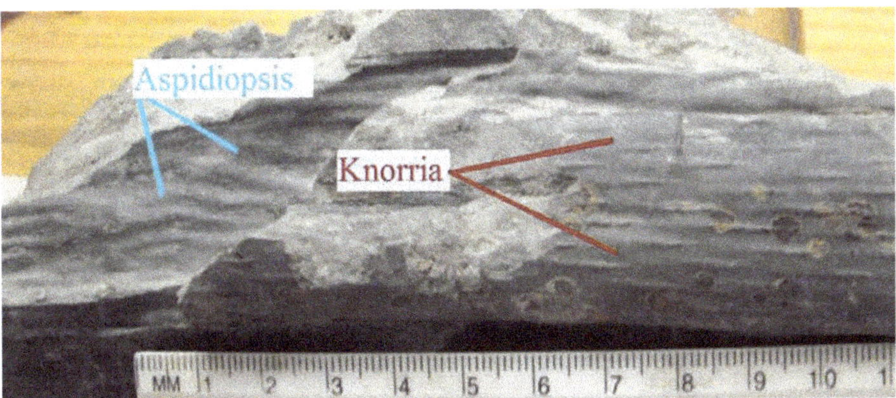

Figure 15: *Fossil collected from the Pardee coal bed horizon 6 miles West of Jct. of Rt. 68 and 160 West (N Inman St.), Appalachia, Wise County, Virginia. Labeled are the exposed bark layers.*

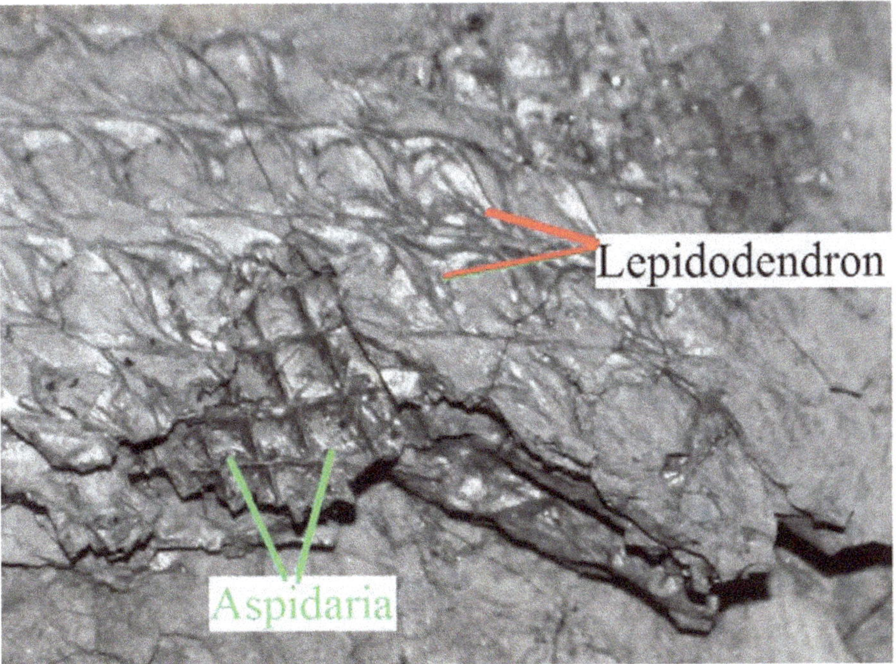

Figure 16: Species of Lepidodendron are based on the pattern and morphology of the leaf cushions on the surface (bark). See fossil shown above marked Lepidodendron as one example of the leaf cushions that was found 1 mile North of Stonega West off State Route 78, Wise County, Virginia.

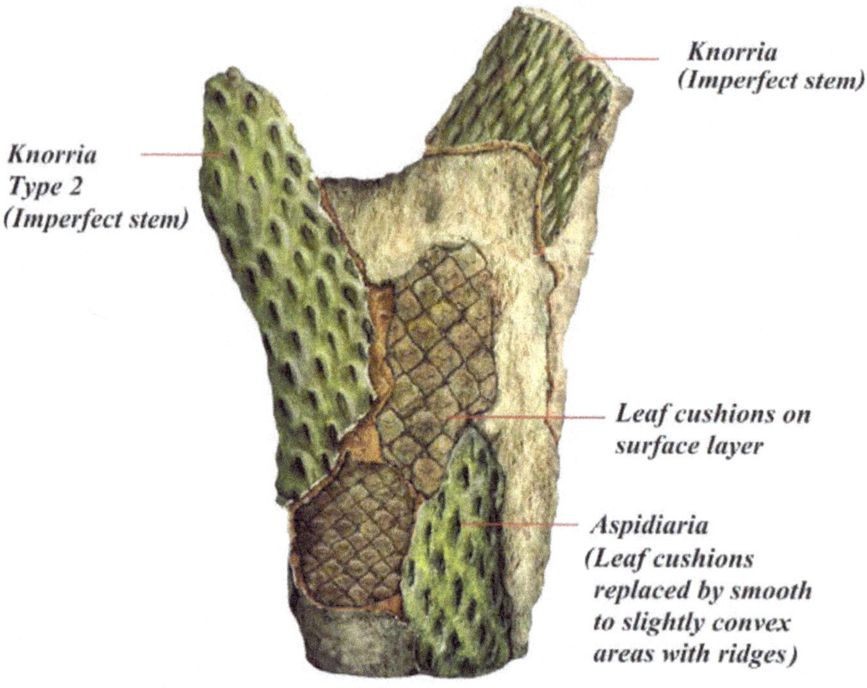

Figure 17: *Another illustration of the different stages of decay (decortication) of Lepidodendron. Modified after Seward, 1889, volume. 11, figure 156, page 125. Colorization courtesy of Jon Hughes/ www.jfhdigital.com.*

PLATE I *Lepidodendron* –1, 1a. *Lepidodendron sp.-Syringodendron Lepidodendron* in the stage of *Knorria*. 3. *Lepidophloios* Collected from the strata above the Pardee coal bed 6 miles West of Jct. of Rt. 68 and 160 West (N Inman St.) Appalachia, Wise County, Viginia.

PLATE II *Lepidodendron* –1, 2. *Lepidodendron sporophyte* (small branch) 3. *Lepidostrobo- phylum* 4. *Lepidodendron* showing wood layers *Knorria* and *Aspidiopsis*. Collected from the strata above the Pardee coal bed 6 miles West of Jct. of Rt. 68 and 160 West (N Inman St.) Appalachia, Wise County, Virginia.

PLATE III *Lepidodendron*–1, 1a, 1b *Lepidodendron obovatum*. 2 and 2a reverse side of specimen in image 1 (First wood layer with leaf scares). Collected by Daniel B. Edwards, a coal miner, from a mine developed in the Imboden coal bed located 1 mile North of Stonega, Wise County, Virginia along State Route 600.

PLATE IV *Lepidodendron* –1, 1a *Lepidodendron The turbinatum*, 2 reverse side of image 1. 3. *Lepidodendron wortheni*. Collected by Brandon Brock, a coal miner, from a mine developed in the Taggart coal bed located 2.5 miles North of Stonega, Wise County, Virginia along State Route 600.

PLATE V *Lepidodendron* –1. *Lepidodendron Knorria*. Collected by Brandon Brock, a coal miner, from a mine developed in the Taggart coal bed located 2.5 miles North of Stonega, Wise County, Virginia along State Route 600.

Plate VI *Lepidodendron* –1. *Lepidostrobus* (reproductive cone). Collected above the Dorchester coal bed 2 miles North of the Junction Route 624 and 83 near Georges Fork, Dickenson County, Virginia. 2. *Lepidodendron rigens*. Collected from the Imboden coal bed at Osaka, Wise County, Virginia

Plate VII *Lepidodendron*–1. *Lepidophylloides?* (branch with attached leaves) collected from the Pardee coal bed horizon located 6 miles West of Junction Route 68 and 160 West (N Inman Street) Appalachia, Wise County, Virginia. 2. *Lepidodendron mannabachense* with leaves. Specimen collected in Aces Branch North off Lower Macintosh Road (KY-3425) 3.3 miles South East of Dryhill, Leslie County, Kentucky from the Hazard #8(Francis)/#9 (Hidman) coal bed horizons.

PLATE I *Lepidodendron branch*—1. *Lepidodendron* branch in shale. Collected at a strip mine in the Lower Bolling (=Imboden coal seam). Location is 2.8 miles from junction of State Route 364 (Bean Gap Road) and State Route 673 (Hubbard Hollow Road), South of Pound, Wise County, Virginia.

Plate I Lepidodendron

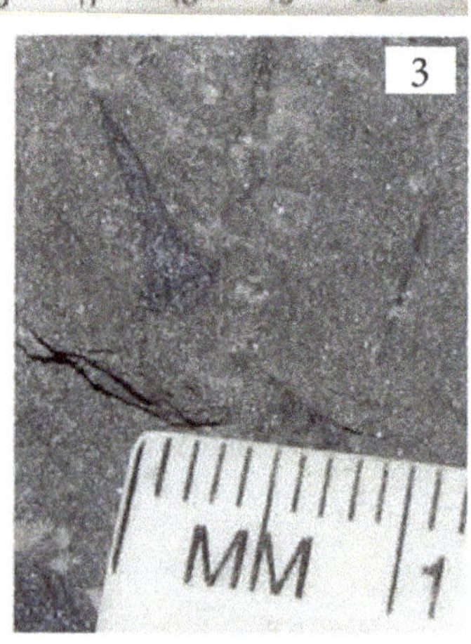

Plate II Lepidodendron

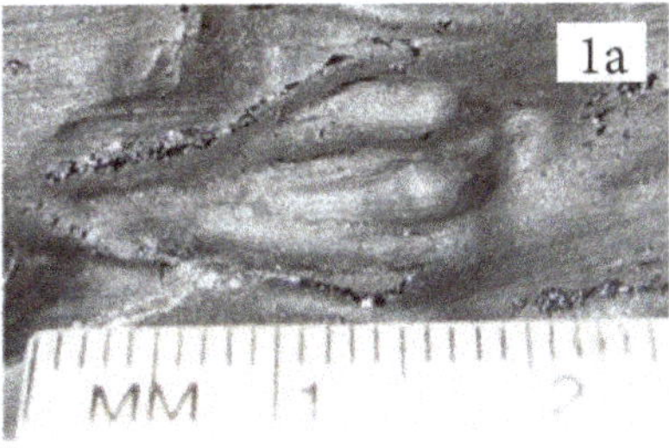

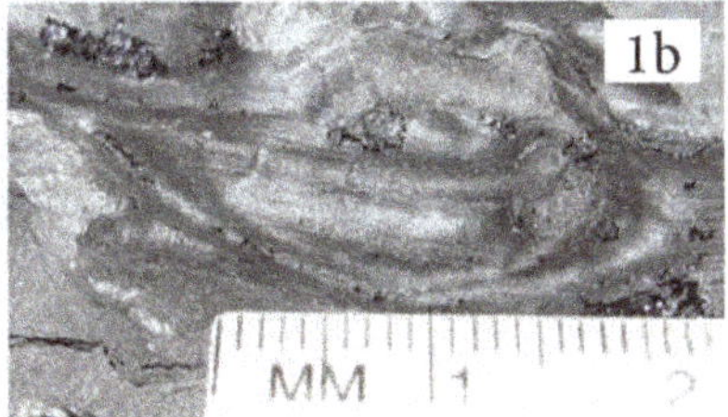

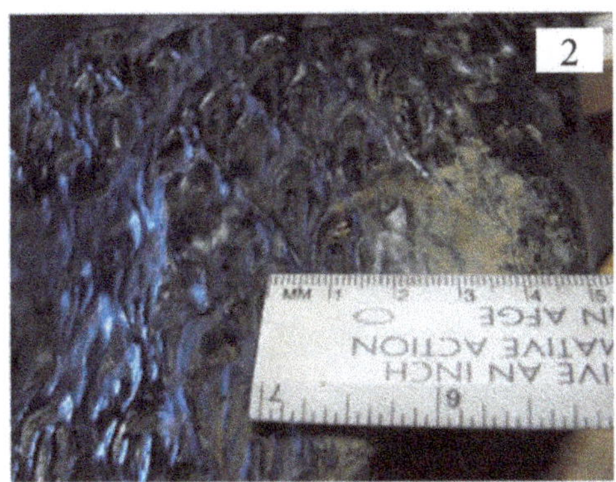

Plate III Lepidodendron

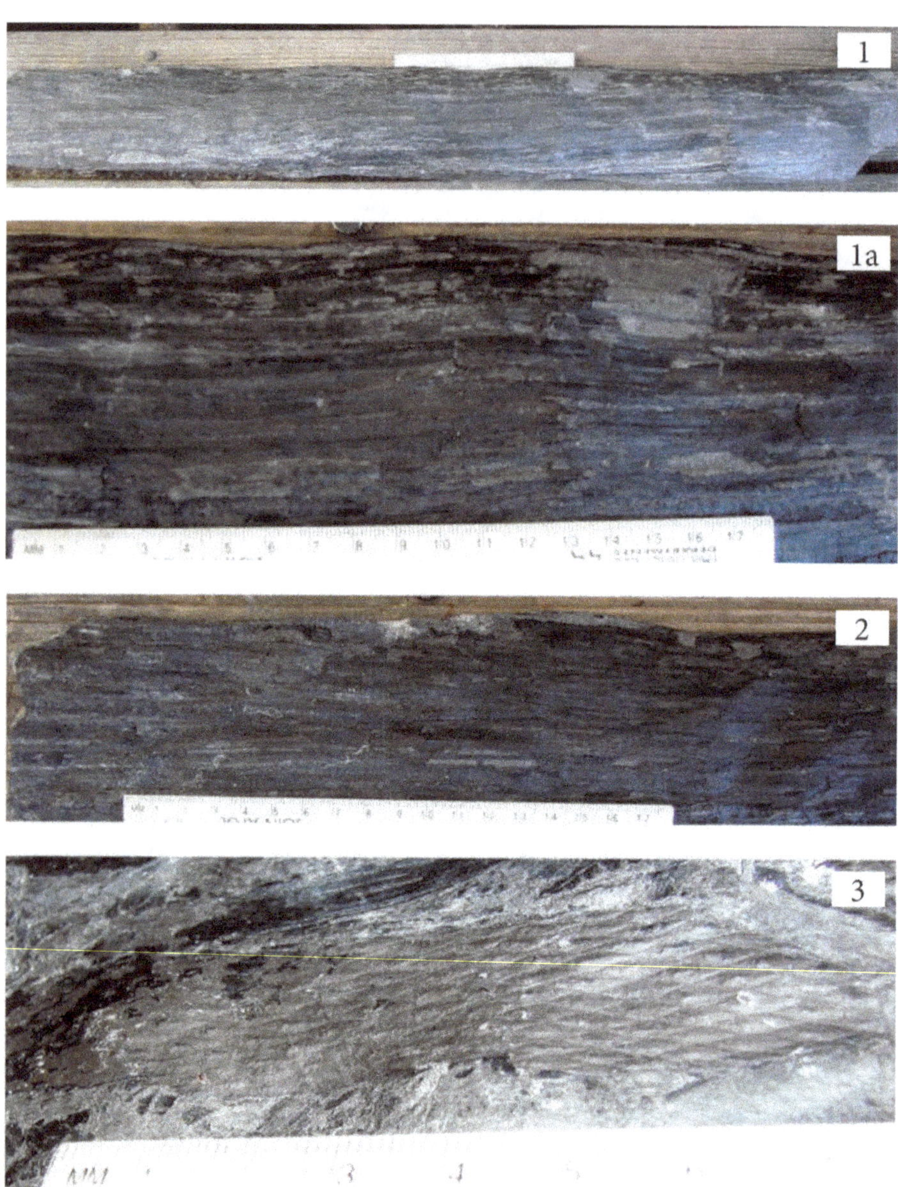

Plate IV Lepidodenron

Plate V Lepidodendron

Plate I Lepidodendron Branch

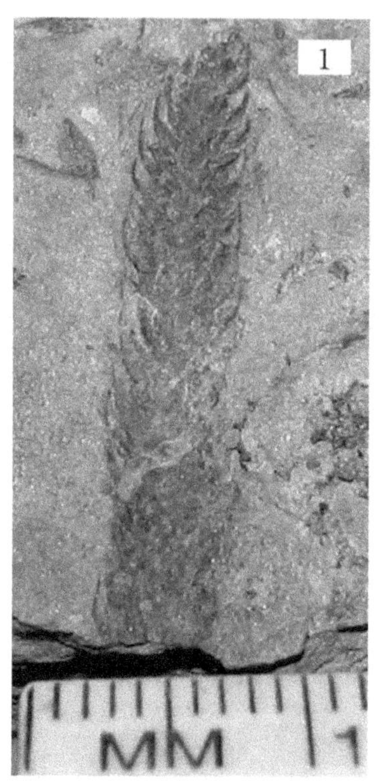

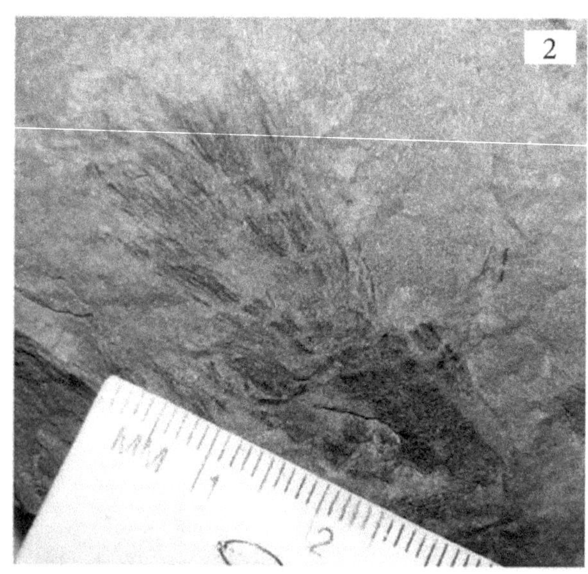

Plate VI Lepidodendron

Plate VII Lepidodendron

PLATE I – *Bergeria* *

1. Bergeria (cryptic leaf scar at very near to the top of the leaf cushion, twig with leaves). Collected by Brandon Brock, a coal miner, from a mine developed in the Taggart coal bed located 2.5 miles North of Stonega, Wise County, Virginia along State Route 600.

* Wagner, Robert and Carmen-Álvarez-Vázquez, (2014)

Plate I Bergeria

BOTHRODENDRON

PLATE I–*Bothrodendron*

1. *Bothrodendron sp.* collected from the Pardee coal bed horizon located 6 miles West of Junction Route 68 and 160 West (N Inman Street) Appalachia, Wise County, Virginia. 2. *Bothrodendron punctatum* collected from the Hazard #9 coal bed horizon 2.8 miles off Route 421 approximately 4 miles West of Hyden, Leslie County, Kentucky.

Plate I Bothrodendron

PLATE I–*Lycophyta* foliage

1. 1a Collected 0.3 miles East of Vicco, Perry County, Kentucky along I-15 at the Knott and Perry County boarder above the Upper Whitesburgh coal bed in a road cut. 2,3 Vergie, Pike County, Kentucky. 4. "Asparagus fern".

Plate I Lycophyta foliage

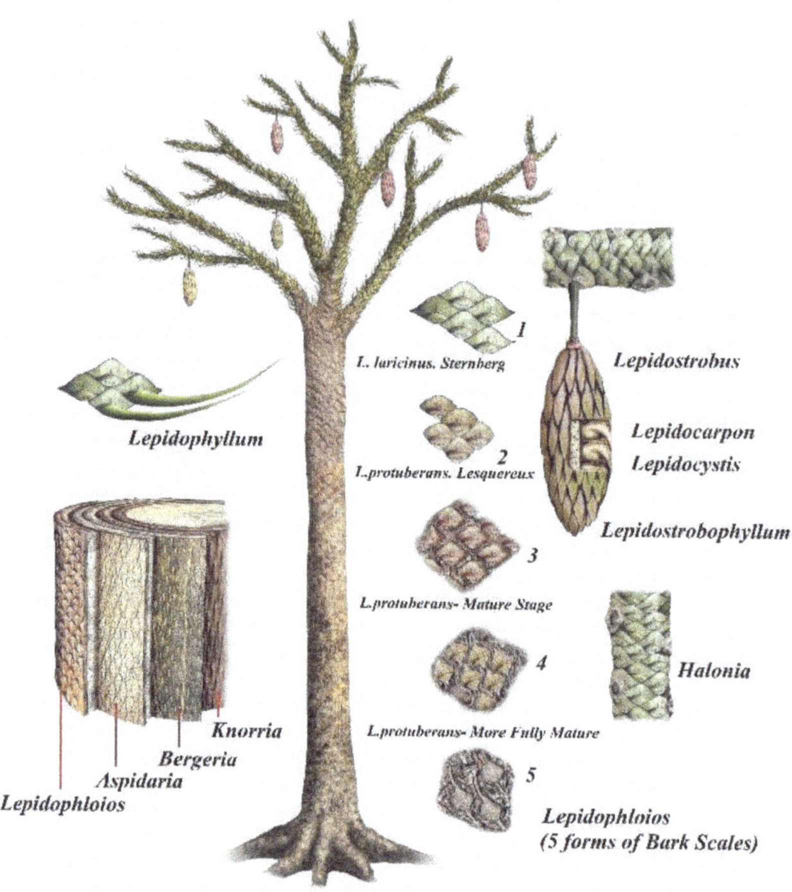

Figure 18: *Lepidophloios and it parts. The generic name means "scale bark." It is similar to Lepidodendron. The main difference between these two genera in compression preservation is that Lepidophloios leaf cushions are wide than high, and 2) imbricate – they protrude and overlap like shingles. Anatomically, they are very different and clearly differentiable (B. DiMichele personal communication). Modified after Longford, G., 1958, figure 130, page 77 by permission of Esconi Associates, Illinois. Colorization courtesy of Jon Hughes/ www.jfhdigital.com.*

PLATE I – *Lepidophloios*

1, 1a *Lepidophloios protuberans* small stem. Note the generic name *Lepidophloios* means "scale bark" (Langford, G., 1958). Collected from the Pocahontas #2 coal seam State Route 77 2.8 miles South of Flat Top, Mercer County, West Virginia

PLATE I – *Lepidophloios Holonia*

1, 1a, 1b *Holonia tortuosa.* Specimens collected by Keith Lawson of Hyden, Kentucky. It was found at a strip mine where the Hazard #8(Francis)/#9 (Hidman) coal beds are mined in Aces Branch North off Lower Macintosh Rd. (KY-3425) 3.3 miles South East of Dryhill, Leslie County, Kentucky.

PLATE II – *Lepidostrobus*

1. *Lepidostrobus ovatifolius.* Specimen collected in Aces Branch North off Lower Macintosh Rd. (KY- 3425) 3.3 miles South East of Dryhill, Leslie County, Kentucky from the Hazard #8(Francis)/#9 (Hidman) coal bed horizons.

2. *Lepidostrobophyllum* collected from the Williamson coal bed horizon approximately 5 miles Southeast of Sideny, Pike County, Kentucky along U.S. Route 119.

Plate III – *Lepidodendron* and *Sigillaria* Reproductive Organs

1. *Lepidostrobus sp.* in shale. Collected at a strip mine in the Lower Bolling (=Imboden coal seam). Location is 2.8 miles from junction of State Route 364 (Bean Gap Road) and State Route 673 (Hubbard Hollow Road), South of Pound, Wise County, Virginia.

2. *Lepidostrobus, sp.* in sandstone. Collected at a strip mine in the Lower Bolling (=Imboden Coal seam). Location is 2.8 miles from junction of State Route 364 (Bean Gap Road) and State Route 673 (Hubbard Hollow Road), South of Pound, Wise County, Virginia.

Plate I Lepidophloios

Plate I Lepidophloios Halonia

Plate I Lepidostrobus

1   2

Plate III Lepidodendron & Sigillaria Reproductive Organs

PLATE I–*Lepidodendris*

1. *Lepidodendris* stem 1a subsurface layer. The elongate dashes are the leaf traces and continuous lines probably represent some type of ribs or thick-walled tissue in the bark. (Description of specimen taken from the Arizona Atate University Department of Plan Biology website). Collected by Brandon Brock, a coal miner, from a mine developed in the Taggart coal bed located 2.5 miles North of Stonega, Wise County, Virginia along State Route 600.

1

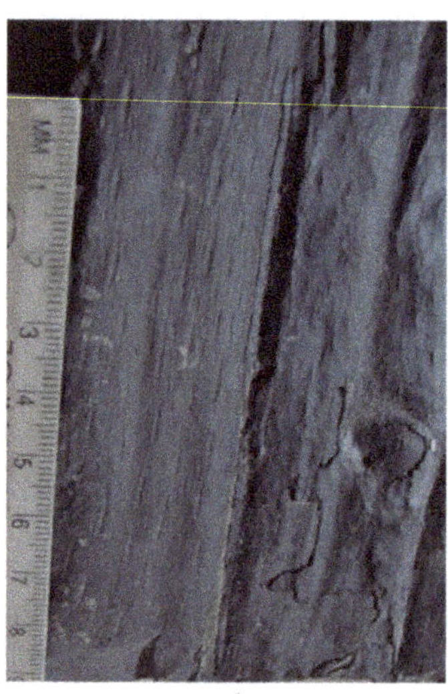

1a

Plate II Lepidodendris

ULODENDRON

Figure 19: *Sketch of a Bergeria tree by permission of Dinoera.com (originally labeled Ulodendron) and modified from Langford, G., 1876. Change based on personal communication with William (Bill) DiMichele. Colorization courtesy of Jon Hughes/ www.jfhdigital. com.*

Ulodendron is the genus name for a species of fossil tree (lycopod) stem that was once thought to be a part of *Lepidodendron* (B.A. Thomas, 1968). On one occasion while inspecting an underground coal mine I observed several Ulodendrons laying side by side and where at least 20 feet in length. I could not get a picture because of where I was in the mine and the roof was too low. The roof rock was so hard I could not get a sample. Langford, (1876) described it as having large branch scars in two vertical rows, one row opposite the other as shown in drawing above Figure 19). The specimen shown below was first thought to be a genus of Ulodendron. However, William A. DiMichele, PhD. of the Department of Paleobiology at the Smithsonian National Museum of Natural History byper-sonal communication, believes that the "*Ulodendron*" with the large branching scars fit into the sister genus *Diaphorodendron* or *Synchysidendron*. As part of the *Diaphorodendraceae* family, these were big trees with branch, as well as leaf, abscission (i.e. the natural detachment of parts of a plant, typically dead leaves and ripe repro-duction pods).

Figure 20: *Diaphorodendraceae. This specimen was collected by Brandon Brock, a coal miner, from a mine developed in the Taggart coal bed located 2.5 miles North of Stonega, Wise County, Virginia along State Route 600.*

CHAPTER 2

ABORESCENT LYCOPODS (CLUB MOSSES)

SIGILLARIA

Another club moss tree, SIGILLARIA (Figure 21), along with its relative Lepidodendron, were among the most common and most widespread floras of Europe and North America. Both club mosses belong to the lycopod class (Lycopsida). These trees dom-inated the Carboniferous up to the Middle–Late Pennsylvanian boundary. Progressively smaller forms existed through the Mesozoic era with the last surviving member of the group considered to be the modern quillwort (Isoetes). Sigillaria and Lepidodendron were differentiated by the pattern and morphology of the leaf cushions and scars. The leaf scars and leaf cushions of Sigillaria were oval to hexaginal and did not have the elongate "diamond" shape typical of Lepidodendron. In many Sigillaria species the leaf cushions where arranged in vertical columns in contrast to Lepidodendron where the scars were spirally disbursed along the stems, although in another group the leaf cushions were spirally arranged (and it is one of these forms that survives into the Late Pennsylvanian and Permian). The leaves of *Sigillaria* were long and grass-like leaving roughly hexago-nal scars which sometimes occupy most of the area of the leaf cush-ion, as they were shed. The scars of many species were arranged in vertical columns (See Figure 18). Species are identified on the basis of the shapes of the scars and the patterns of the scars. As a consequence of the vertical orientation of the leaf cushions, in some species the impression of the bark is identified by broad linear ridges that are much wider than those of *Calamites*, and there is no segmentation (See Figure 22). The ridges vary in design from plain to ornamental, with tiny circular depressions resembling bull-seyes. Its leaves and roots are very similar to *Lepidodendron*, but the leaf-cushion shape is different. Figure 23 shows a cast fossil stump of *Sigillaria*. The indentations are the usual parichnos scars arranged in vertical columns associated with this genus.

Figure 21: *Drawing of Sigillaria courtesy of Jon Hughes/www.jfhdigital.com*

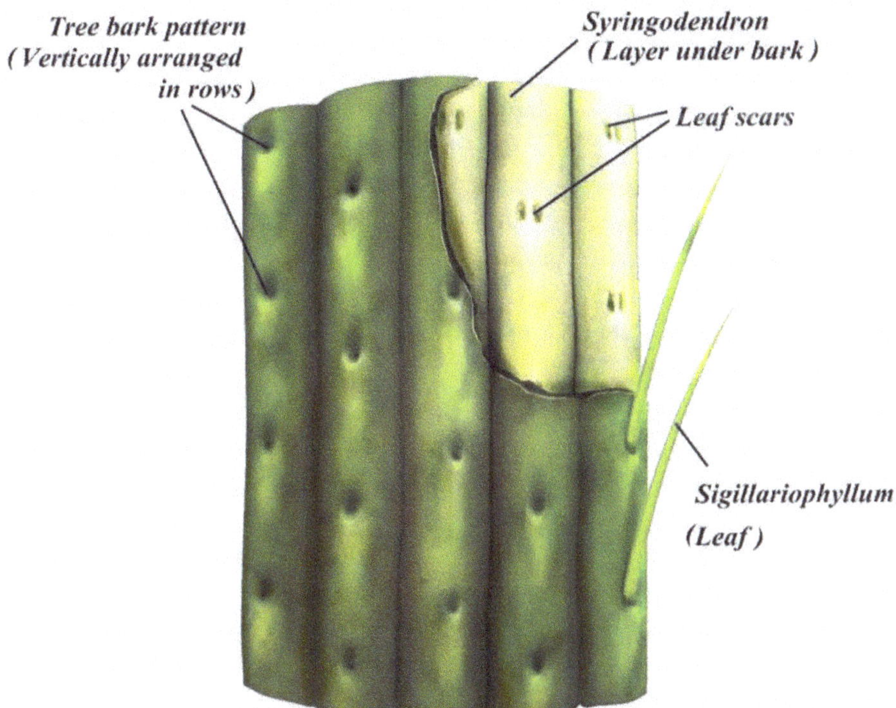

Figure 22: Drawing showing key characteristics of Sigillaria taken from Langford, G., 1958, figure 206, page 113. Colorization courtesy of Jon Hughes/www. jfhdigital.com

Figure 23: Partial cast fossil stump of Sigillaria. The indentations are the usual parichnos scars arranged in vertical columns associated with this genus.

PLATE I–*Sigillaria*

1. Section of tree trunk of *Sigillaria sp.* Collected from the Taggart Marker between Keeoke and Appalachia, Lee-Wise Counties, Virginia. 2. *Sigillaria cf ichthyolepis* col-lected 5.8 miles Northwest of Inman, Wise County, VA on State Route 160.

Plate I Sigillaria

CHAPTER 3

CALAMITES
(HORSE TAIL RUSHES)

CALAMITES (Figure 24) are the extinct ancestors of the modern sphenophytes (horsetails). A comparison of the outward appearances between Calamites and horsetails is shown in McLoughlin, 2017. The basic anatomy of the Calamites is shown in figure 25. Unlike its living relative, Calamites grew to the size of small trees. Its main stalk or trunk has a bamboo-like appearance characterized by being segmented (jointed) at intervals with finely spaced grooves oriented parallel to the long axis of the plant. The rib patterns of the preserved stem casts where they meet at the nodal line are used to group the genera and subgenera of Calamites (See Figure 26). Along the joint, one can see radial scars where smaller branches split off of the main stem. Specimens in which the ribs alternate are true Calamites; ribs that have some alternating with others passing through the node are assigned to the subgenus Mesocalamites (See McLoughlin,T.F., 2017). Calamites stem characteristics or patterns are illustrated in figure 28. Figure 27 is an artist reconstruction of a portion of the main truck of Calamites showing detail of internal structure (features of inner bark). A generalized diagram of the root system is shown in figure 27. The leaves, which resemble pedals on a flower, are distributed in a circular (or whorled) pattern around the stems at evenly spaced intervals, somewhat resembling a pinwheel. Specimens with leaves that are linear, lanceolate, or spatulate are referred to as *Annularia*. Their bases form a collar around the stem but could be absent from some fossils; they have leaves in whorls of 5–32 per node. *Asterophyllites* have leaves that are longer and nar-rower than those from *Annularia*. These leaves are not united at the bases and have whorls of 4 to 40 per node; they arch steeply upward from the stem.

Figure 24: *An original reconstruction of a grove of Calamites courtesy of Jon hughes/www.jfhdigital.com.*

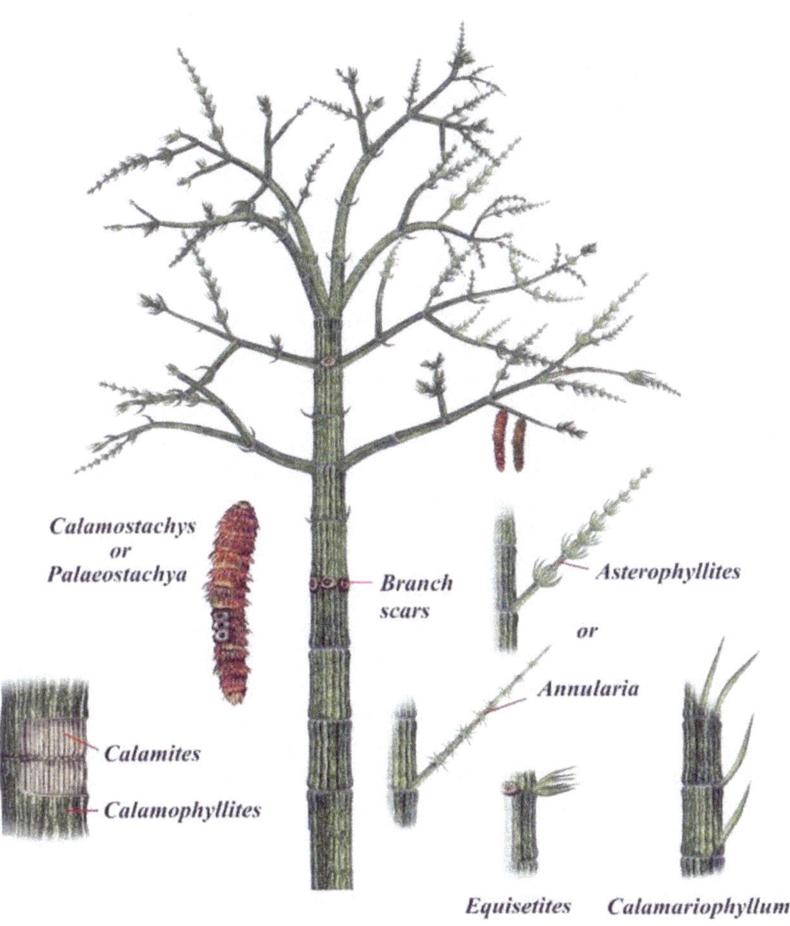

Figure 25: *Calamites and its parts modified from Langford, G., 1958, figure 18, page 29 by permission of Esconi Associates, Illinois. Colorization courtesy of Jon Hughes/www.jfhdigital.com*

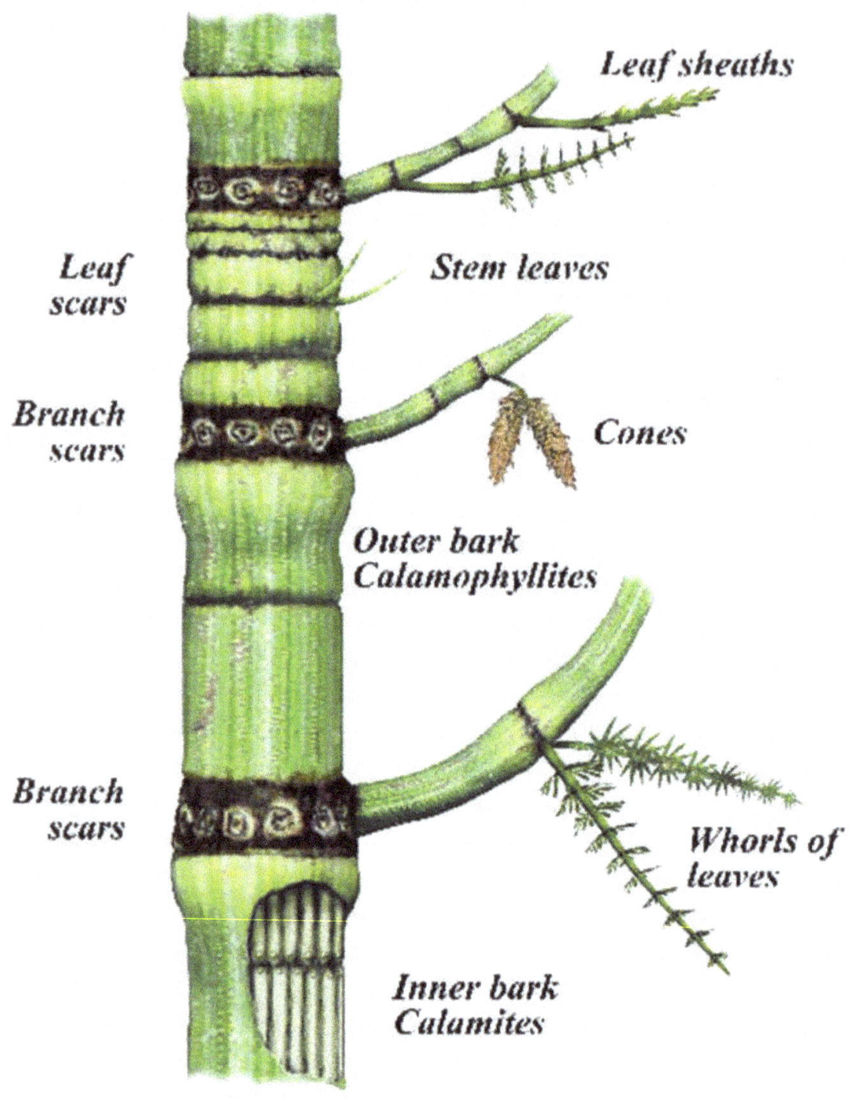

Figure 26: *Diagram of a trunk section of Calamites showing the various elements that are found as fossils (Langford, G., 1876). Colorization courtesy of Jon Hughes/www.jfhdigital.com.*

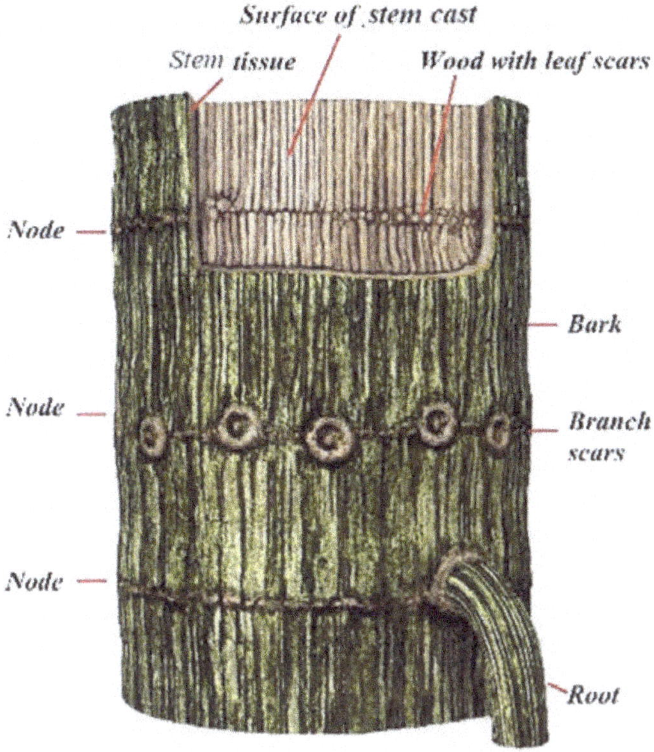

Figure 27: *Artist reconstruction of a portion of the main truck of Calamites showing detail of internal struc-ture (features of inner bark). Modified from Seward, A.C. 1898, Volume I, figure 77, page 316. Colorization courtesy of Jon Hughes/www.jfhdigital.com.*

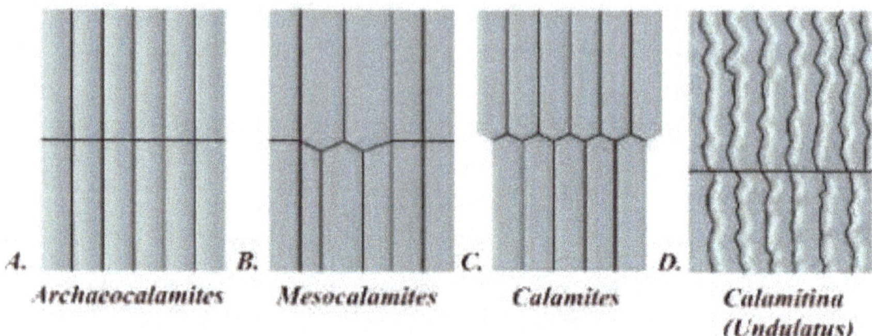

Figure 28: *Calamites stem characteristics A through D are used to identify the general genera. Modified from Gillespie et al., 1978. Colorization courtesy of Jon Hughes/www.jfhdigital.com.*

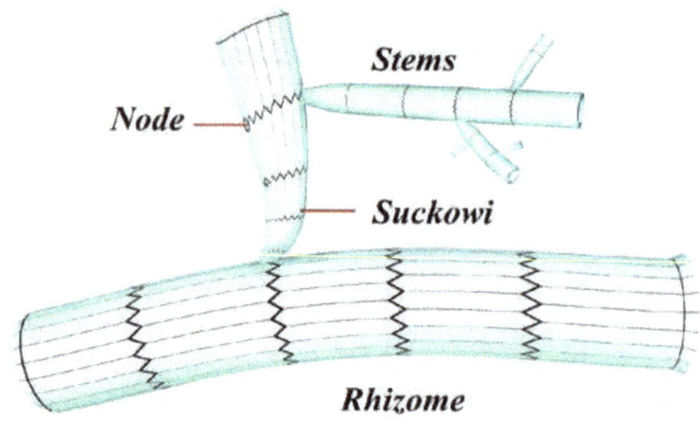

Figure 29: *Reconstruction of the root system and attached parts of Calamites by permission of and mod-ified after Hans Star, 2017, www.fossieleplanten.*

PLATE I *Calamites*–1 *Calamites suckowi* (base of a stem). 1b Reconstructed to show tapering at point of attachment to trunk of the plant. 2. *Calamites carinatus?* (pith cast). 3. *Calamities sp.*, 3a. Preserved outer bark of *Calamites*, *Calamophyllites* 3b Carbonized outer bark layer of *Calamites*. Collected by Brandon Brock, a coal miner, from a mine developed in the Taggart coal bed located 2.5 miles North of Stonega, Wise County, Virginia along State Route 600. 4. *Calamites sp.* preserved in pyrite collected from the Taggart Marker coal bed located 1.6 miles Northwest off Route 78 and 1 mile from Stonega, Wise County, Virginia. 5 Cross section of a stem of *Calamites* show-ing the diaphragm and vascular strands radiating from the core. The vascular strains are expressed on the surface of the plant as ribs. Specimen collected from the Pocahontas No. 3 coal bed from a shaft mine, approximately 1500 feet below the surface, near Keen Mountain, Buchanan County, Virginia.

PLATE II *Calamites*–1,1a *Calamites undulates* collected from the Imboden coal bed 1.3 miles North of Stonega, Wise County, Virginia. 2 *Calamitina* collected from above the Kennedy coal bed 1.5 miles South of Pilgroms Knob on State Route 680 on Saw Mill road, Buchanan County, Virginia.

PLATE III *Calamites*–1. *Calamites suckowi* collected from the roof in a coal mine developed in the Kellioka coal bed near Homes Mill, Harlan County, Kentucky. 2,2a *Calamites* cross section at node showing leaf scares looking down long axis. Specimen collected from above the Norton coal bed located 0.3 miles North of the Jct. of Rt. 623 and 624 Georges Fork, Dickenson County, Virginia. *Calamites ramifer* Stur, 1875, with branch scare collected from the Taggart Marker coal bed horizon located 1.6 miles Northwest off Route 78 and 1 mile from Stonega, Wise County, Virginia. 4. Calamites *schützei-formis* collected from an "unnamed" coal seam along a railroad right of way parallel to the westbound lane along Route 58 in Appalachia, Wise County, Virginia.

PLATE IV *Calamites*–1 *Calamites multiramus* with *calamites* foliage. 2. *Calamites suckowi* with foliage. Both specimens collected in Aces Branch North off Lower Macintosh Rd. (KY-3425) 3.3

miles South East of Dryhill, Leslie County, Kentucky from the Hazard #8(Francis)/#9 (Hidman) coal bed horizons. 3, 3a *Calamites undulates* with *Calamites goeppertii*. Collected from immediately above Splashdam coal bed 2.5 miles East of Haysi, Dickenson County, Virginia along Route 83 (Dickenson Highway) 0.4 miles from the Junction of Route 83 and 680.

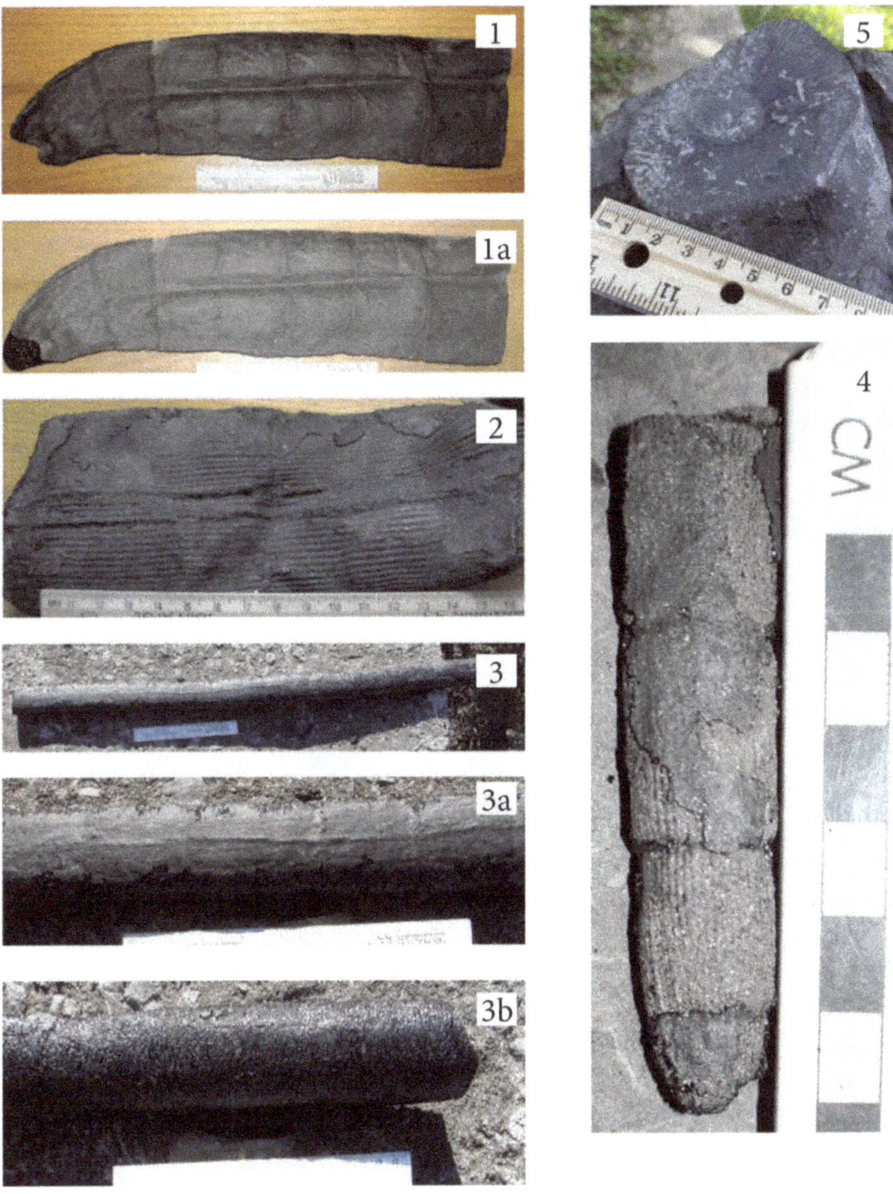

Plate I *Calamites*

Plate II *Calamites*

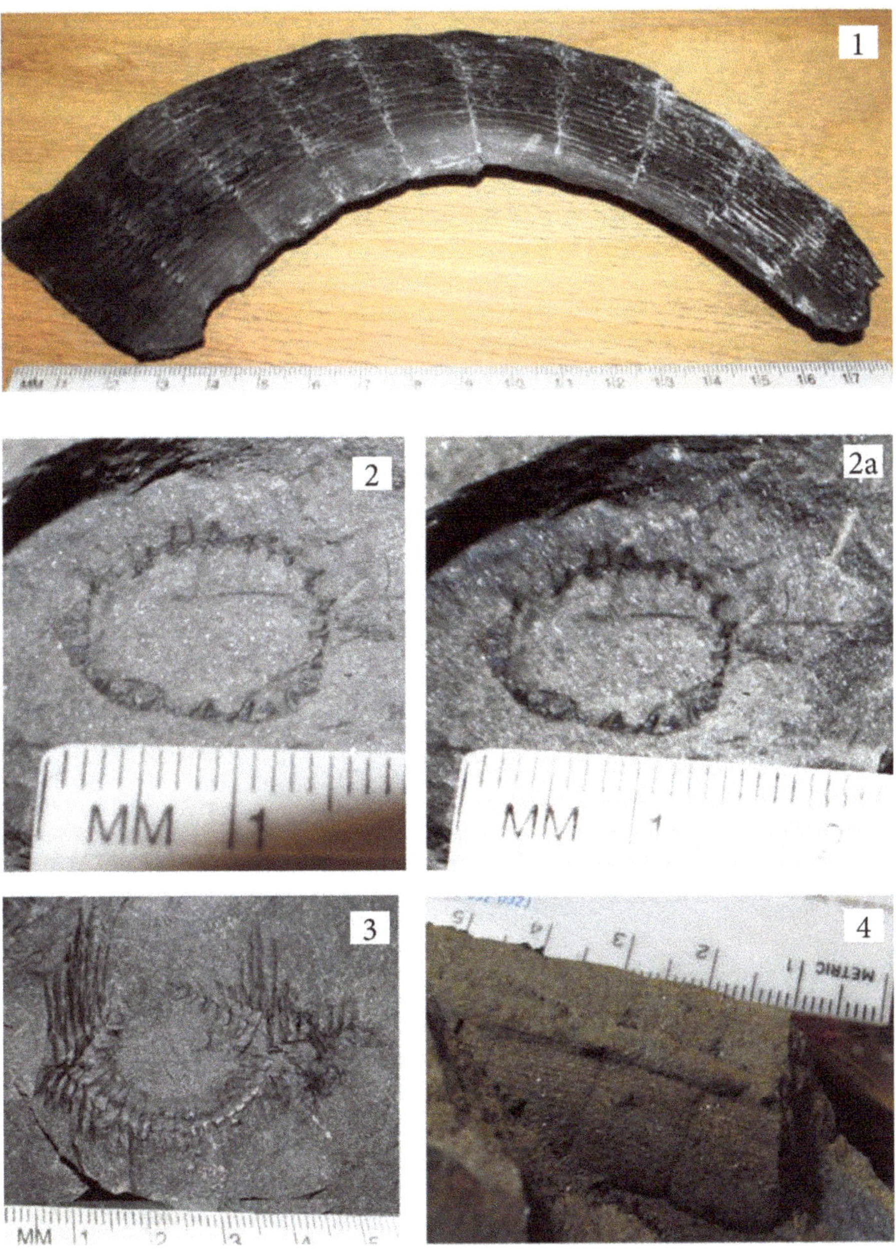

Plate III *Calamites*

Plate IV Calamites

PLATE I *Calamites* Foliage–1. *Annularia radiata*. 2. *Annularia asteris*. 3 *Asterophyllities charaefomis*. Collected from strata immediately above the Kenney coal bed, 1.5 miles South of Pilgrims Knob on State Route 680 on Saw Mill Road, Buchanan County, Virginia. 4. *Annularia spicata*. Collected from above the Pardee coal bed 6 miles West of the Junction Route 68 and 160 West (N. Inman Street), Appalachia, Wise County, Virginia. 5. *Annularia radiate* collected from a road cut located 3.1 miles South of Junction Routes 23 and 805, 1.1 miles South of Myra, Pike County, Kentucky

PLATE II *Calamites* Foliage–1 *Annularia radiate* collected directly above the Norton coal bed located 0.3 miles North of the Junction of Routes 623 and 624, near Georges Fork, Dickinson County, Virginia.

PLATE III *Calamites* Foliage–1,1a *Asterophyllites equisetiformis* (Schlotheim) Brongniart 2. *Annularia sphenophylloides*. Both specimens collected by Keith Lawson of Hyden, Kentucky. It was found at a strip mine where the Hazard #8(Francis)/#9 (Hidman) coal beds are mined in Aces Branch North off Lower Macintosh Rd. (KY-3425) 3.3 miles South East of Dryhill, Leslie County, Kentucky.

PLATE I *Calamites* Roots–1,1a *Pinnularia (Myriophyllites)* collected directly above the Norton coal bed located 0.3 miles North of the Junction of Routes 623 and 624, near Georges Fork, Dickinson County, Virginia. 2. *Pinnularia (Myriophyllites)* collected from the Dorchester coal bed horizon located 2 miles North of the Junction of Routes 624 and 83 near Georges Fork, Dickenson County, Virginia.

PLATE I *Calamites* Reproductive Cones–1. *Calamostachys*. It was found at a strip mine where the Hazard #8(Francis)/#9 (Hidman) coal beds are mined in Aces Branch North off Lower Macintosh Rd. (KY-3425) 3.3 miles South East of Dryhill, Leslie County, Kentucky. 2. *Calamostachys schimper*. It was col-lected above an undefined coal bed located 0.5 miles North of Belfrey, Pike County, KY along Route 119.

Plate I *Calamites Foliage*

Plate II *Calamites Foliage*

Plate III *Calamites Foliage*

Plate I *Calamites Reproductive Cones*

Plate I *Calamites Roots*

CHAPTER 4

SPHENOPHYLLUM

SPHENOPHYLLUM is a genus of small, vine-like, and bramble-like land plants possessing characteristics that could be mistaken for the whorl from Calamites foliage, but typically smaller than *Annularia* or *Asterophyllites* and unlike calamitalean foliage, in which leaves are single veined, has multiple veins per leaf. The stems were jointed and longitudinally ribbed. The foliage consisted of whorls of leaves that were triangular shaped and rounded or forked at the apex. Most likely they resembled the modern ground covering (bed straw) plant *Galium*. Reconstructions of the plant by a drawing and a model are presented in Figure 30 and Figure 31, respectively.

Figure 30: Reconstruction of Sphenophyllum of Arden R Bashforth. From R and Zodrow, 2007.

Figure 31: Sphenophyllum emarginatum plant model by permission of © The Field Museum, B83051c, photographer John Bayallis.

PLATE I–*Sphenophyllum*

1. *Sphenophyllum majus* with *Sterophyllites* (top right) Specimen collected from the Dorchester coal bed hori-zon 200 feet North of the Jct. of Roley Fleming Lane & Camp Creek Road 1 mile West of Georges Fork, Dickenson County, Virginia 2. *Sphenophyllym longifo-lium*. 3. *Sphenophyllym longifolium*. Both 2 and 3 col-lected at a strip mine where the Hazard #8(Francis)/#9 (Hidman) coal beds are mined in Aces Branch North off Lower Macintosh Road (KY-3425) 3.3 miles South East of Dryhill, Leslie County, Kentucky.

Plate I *Sphenophyllum*

CHAPTER 5

FERNS AND SEED FERNS

Reconstructions of an extinct seed fern and an exist true fern trees are shown in figure 32. A living tree fern is shown in figure 33.

Figure 32: *Reconstruction of Medullosa, seed fern colorization courtesy of Jon Hughes/www. jfhdigital.com*

Figure 33: *A typical tree fern,* **Cibotium sp***. found on the big island of Hawaii. Photo taken by the author in December 2006.*

Fern Morphology

General classification and naming of ferns are based on a standard, specialized terminology that is used in even the most elementary fi eld guides to fossil ferns. Figure 34 illustrates the basic terms applied to each of the components found in modern ferns; ancient ferns have the same terminology applied to them. Incomplete or fragmented fernlike compound leaves are assigned to the basic form-genera determined by using the general morphology of pinnules, venation, and the way they are attached to the rachis (See Figure 35 and Figure 36). A reference that is highly recommended for indexes to the numerous fern species is Langford, G., (1958.)

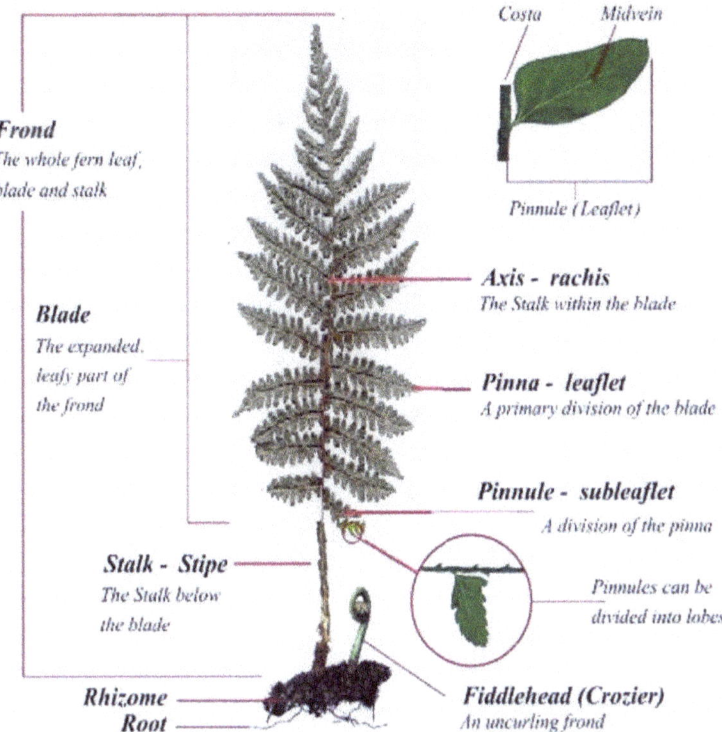

Figure 34: *A general illustration of terms used in describing the morphology of pinnately compound fern frond. Colorization courtesy of Jon Hughes/ www. jfhdigital.com*

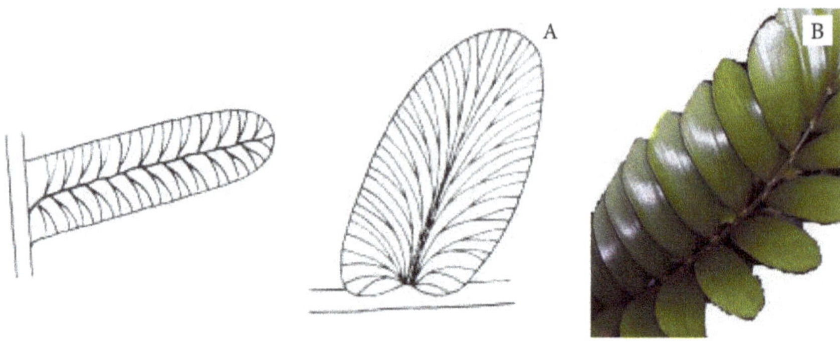

Pecopteris-like: the pinnules are attached to the axis over (nearly) the whole base. Pecopteris, Alloiopteris

Neuropteris-like: the pinnules are attached to the axis in one point. Neuropteris, Neuralethopteris, Reticulopteris, Paripteris,Linopteris(A). Zamia furfuracea (B).Neuropteris-like: the pinnules are attached to the axis in one point. Neuropteris, Neuralethopteris, Reticulopteris, Paripteris,Linopteris (A). Zamia furfuracea (B).

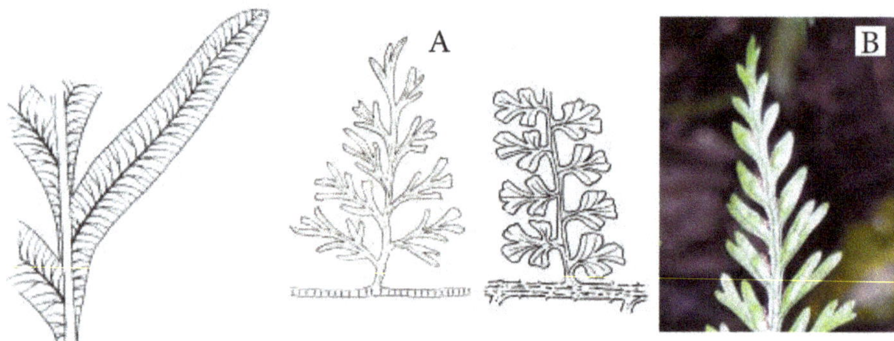

Alethopteris*-like: the pinnules are broadly attached, decurrent along the axis and connected with each other. **Alethopteris Neuralethopteris** have **Neuropturis-like** constricted cordate base, but have **alethopteroid venation**.*

Sphenopteris-like: the pinnules are lobed to deeply incised. Sphenopteris, Palmatopteris, Renaultia, Oligocarpia, Alloiopteris, Fortopteris (A). New Zeland fern Asplenium Lucrosum (B).

Figure 35: *Identification of fernlike fossil pinnules (individual leaflets) and the method of attachment to the central axis (rachis) is the bases for which more specific species can be identified. Also, modern ferns are shown for comparison. After Gothan and Remey, 1957.*

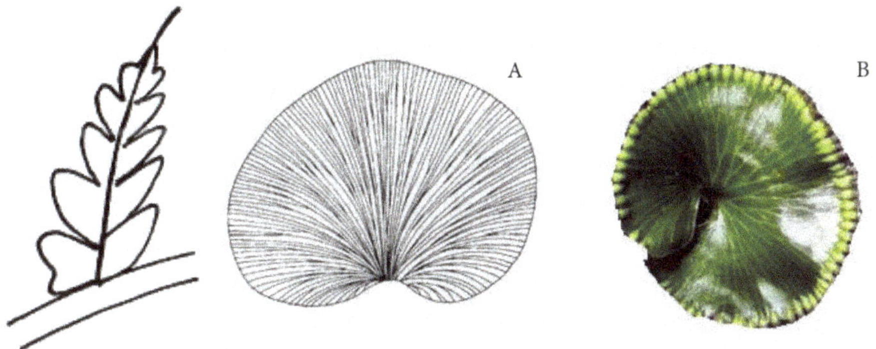

Mariopteris-like: the pinnules are more or less (rounded) triangular. The pinnae have a so-called climbing hook, which is, however, not always visible. After Gothan & Remy, 1957 Mariopteris, Fortopteris

Cyclopteris: (mostly) rounded leaf, which has been attached to the base of a part of a frond. Can be of rather large size (A). After Cleal& Thomas 1994. Kidney fern or Hymenophyllum nephro-phyllum from New Zealand (B).*

Aphlebia: *(part of a) strongly incised leaf. Has been a bract around a young fern leaf. Some species are referred to as Rhacaphyllum by Lesquereux (A). Polypodium falax crested poly fern (B)**. After Gothan & Remy, 1957*

Rhacophyllum: *Similar to* **Cyclopteris** *but with no midvein and has slender veins that do not bifurcate or branch. Also, no evidence of an attachment point (A).* **Adiantum reniforme** *from New Zealand (B)*

*Figure 36: Identification of seed fernlike fossil pinnules (individual leaflets) and the method of attachment to the central axis (rachis) is the basis for which more specific species can be identified. Also, modern ferns are shown how the ancient form may have appeared.. Note: * permission granted by Museum of New Zeland Te Papa Tongarewa. **permission granted by Forest Starr & Kim Starr, Makawao, Hawaii.*

Plate I Seed Fern *Crenulopteris.*

1. *Crenulopteris* Specimens collected immediately above the Amburgy coal bed located 0.6 miles right off State Route 931 and 1.8 miles from the Junction of Route 931 and Route 15 North, Whitesburg, Letcher County, Kentucky.

Plate I Seed Fern Crenulopteris

PLATE I Seed Ferns *Pecopteris*–1.*Pecopteris parvula*.Specimen collected immediately above the Amburgy coal bed located 0.6 miles right off State Route 931 and 1.8 miles from the Junction of Route 931 and Route 15 North, Whitesburg, Letcher County, Kentucky.

PLATE II Seed Ferns *Pectopteris*–1. *Pecopteris taiyuanensis* collected from immediately above the Clintwood/Blair coal beds 1 mile North of the Junction of State Route 83 and Camp Creek Road and 1 mile East of Georges Fork, Dickenson County, Virginia.

PLATE III Seed Ferns *Pecopteris*–1,1a *Pecopteris plumosae* collected by Chris Johnson ("Porky") from the Taggart coal bed hori-zon 1.7 miles West off State Route 624 approximately 0.5 miles North of Junction Routes 624 and 606 near Keokee, Lee County, Virginia. Mr. Johnson, a coal miner from Pound, Virginia gave this fossil to me.

Plate I Seed Ferns Pecopteris

Plate II Seed Ferns Pecopteris

Plate III Seed Fern Pecopteris

PLATE I–Seed Fern *Alethopteris*

1. 1a. *Alethopteris valida* It was found at a strip mine where the Hazard #8(Francis)/#9 (Hidman) coal beds are mined in Aces Branch North off Lower Macintosh Road (KY-3425) 3.3 miles South East of Dryhill, Leslie County, Kentucky.

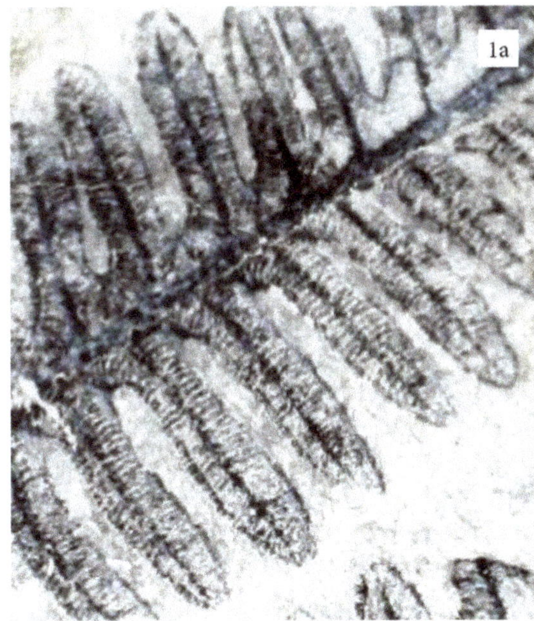

Plate I Seed Ferns Alethopteris

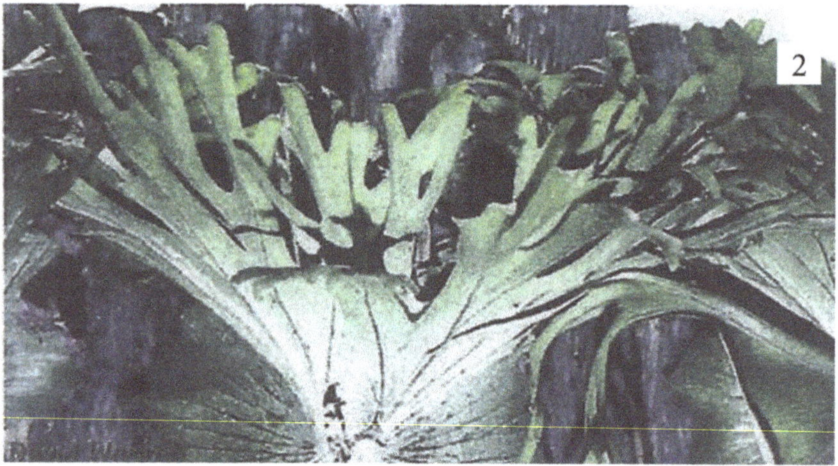

Plate I–Fern *Aphlebia*

1. Aphlebia arborescens collected at a strip mine where the Hazard #8(Francis)/#9 (Hidman) coal beds are mined in Aces Branch North off Lower Macintosh Rd. (KY-3425) 3.3 miles South East of Dryhill, Leslie County, Kentucky.

2. Staghorn fern for comparison. Photo courtesy of Gerald McCormack

Plate I–Seed Fern *Cyclopteris*

1. *Cyclopteris sp.* 2 *Cyclopteris orbicularis.* Both specimens collected from the Hazard #9 coal bed horizon 2.8 miles off Route 421 approximately 4 miles West of Hyden, Leslie County, Kentucky.

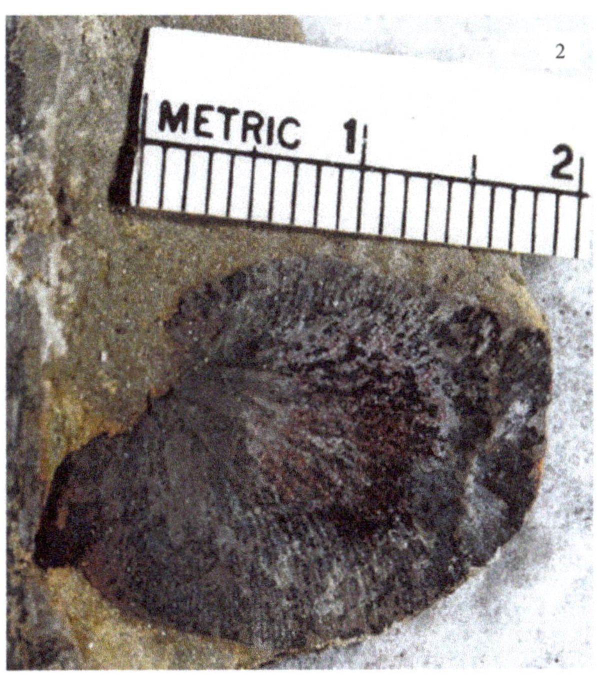

PLATE I–Herbaceous Fern *Alloiopteris*

1. 1a *Alloiopteris coalloides*. Collected just above the Taggart coal bed about 2 miles North of Stonega, Wise County, Virginia.

Plate I Herbaceous Fern Alloiopteris

PLATE I Seed Fern *Sphenopteris*–1, 1. *Sphenopteris souichii* collected just above the Taggart coal bed about 2 miles North of Stonega, Wise County, Virginia.

PLATE II Seed Fern *Sphenopteris*–1. *Sphenopteris crossotheca schat-ziarensis*. Collected from above the Kennedy coal bed 1.5 miles South of Pilgrims Knob on State Route 680 on Saw Mill Road, Buchanan County, Virginia. 2. *Spenopteris sp*. Collected from the Dorchester coal bed horizon approximately 200 feet North of the Junction of Roley Fleming Lane and Camp Creek Road 3 miles West of Georges Fork, Dickenson County, Virginia.

PLATE III Seed Fern *Sphenopteris*–1. *Palmatopteris furcate* collected from an unclassified coal bed on Route 468 just North of Sidney, Pike County, Kentucky. 1a modern fern shown for comparison. 2, 2a *Sphenopteris adiantoides* Collected from above the Kennedy coal bed 1.5 miles South of Pilgrims Knob on State Route 680 on Saw Mill Road, Buchanan County, Virginia.

PLATE IV Seed Fern *Sphenopteris*–1. *Sphenopteris sp*. Collected immediately above the Norton coal bed 0.3 miles North of the Junction of Route 623 and 624 Georges Fork, Dickenson County, Virginia.

PLATE V Seed Fern *Sphenopteris*–1. *Sphenopteris sp*. 2. Sphenopteris neuropteroides. Both specimens collected from 0.3 miles East of Vicco, Perry County, Kentucky along I-15 at the Knott and Perry County boarder above the Upper Whitesburg coal bed.

Plate VI Seed Fern *Sphenopteris*–1,1a *Sphenopteris sp*. Collected from the Hazard #9 coal bed horizon located 2.8 miles off Route 421 approximately 4 miles West of Hyden, Leslie County, Kentucky.

Plate VII Seed Fern *Sphenopteris*–1. *Sphenopteris obtusiloba* Collected from the Taggart Marker coal bed horizon 1.6 miles northwest off Route 78, 1 mile from Stonega, Wise County, Virginia. 2,2a *Sphenopteris sp*. and 3. *Sphenopteris sewardii* collected at a strip mine where the Hazard #8(Francis)/#9 (Hidman) coal beds are mined in Aces Branch North off Lower

Macintosh Rd. (KY- 3425) 3.3 miles South East of Dryhill, Leslie County, Kentucky. 4. *Sphenopteris sp.* Collected from an unclassified coal bed 0.05 miles East of Junction I-119 and Charlie White LN approximately 3 miles East of Millestone, Letcher County, Kentucky.

Plate VIII Seed Fern *Sphenopteris*–1. *Sphenopteris sp.*, 2. *Sphenopteris obtusiloba*, 3. *Sphenopteris sp.* All specimens col-lected from above the Splashdam coal bed in a road cut located Route 83 (Dickenson HWY) 0.4 miles East from Route 680 and 2.5 miles East of Haysi, Dickenson County, Virginia. 4. *Sphenopteris sp.* collected from above the Upper Whitesburg coal bed road cut located 0.3 miles East of Vicco, Perry County, Kentucky along I-15 at the Knott and Perry County boarder.

Plate IX Seed Fern *Sphenopteris* – 1. *Sphenopteris sp.* collected at a strip mine where the Hazard #8(Francis)/#9 (Hidman) coal beds are mined in Aces Branch North off Lower Macintosh Road (KY- 3425) 3.3 miles South East of Dryhill, Leslie County, Kentucky.

Plate I Seed Fern Sphenopteris

Plate II Seed Fern Sphenopteris

Plate III Seed Fern Sphenopteris

Plate IV Seed Fern Sphenopteris

Plate V Seed Fern Sphenopteris

Plate VI Seed Fern Sphenopteris

Plate VII Seed Fern Sphenopteris

Plate VIII Seed Fern Sphenopteris

Plate IX Seed Fern Sphenopteris

PLATE I–Seed Fern *Eremopteris*

1. *Eremopteris artimisiaefolia*. Specimen collected at a strip mine where the Hazard #8(Francis)/#9 (Hidman) coal beds are mined in Aces Branch North off Lower Macintosh Road (KY-3425) 3.3 miles South East of Dryhill, Leslie County, Kentucky.

Plate I Seed Fern Eremopteris

PLATE I Seed Fern *Mariopteris*–1. *Mariopteris muricata*. 2. *Mariopteris sphenopteroides*. Specimens collected from the Taggart Marker coal bed horizon located 1.6 miles northwest off Route 78 and 1 mile North of Stonega, Wise County, Virginia. 3,3a *Mariopteris muricata* collected from the mine roof in a mine developed in the Taggart coal bed approximately 1000 feet left off Route 160 3 miles northwest of the Junction Routes 160W and Route 68, Appalachia, Wise County, Virginia.

PLATE II Seed Fern *Mariopteris*–1, 1a. *Mariopteris acuta* Brongniart. Note the needle like tips as shown by the red arrows. Specimen collected at a strip mine where the Hazard #8(Francis)/#9 (Hidman) coal beds are mined in Aces Branch North off Lower Macintosh Road (KY-3425) 3.3 miles South East of Dryhill, Leslie County, Kentucky.

PLATE III Seed Fern *Mariopteris*–1. *Mariopteris dernoncourti*. Collected at an unclassified coal bed. Road cut 0.05 miles East of Junction I-119 and Charlie White LN approximately 3 miles East of Millestone, Letcher County, Kentucky.

1

2

3

3a

Plate I Seed Fern Mariopteris

Plate II Seed Fern Mariopteris

Plate III Seed Fern Mariopteris

PLATE I—Seed Fern *Karinopteris*

1. *Karinopteris robusta.* Specimen collected at a strip mine where the Hazard #8(Francis)/#9 (Hidman) coal beds are mined in Aces Branch North off Lower Macintosh Road (KY-3425) 3.3 miles South East of Dryhill, Leslie County, Kentucky.

Plate I Seed Fern Karinopteris

PLATE I True Fern *Boweria*–1. *Boweria sp.* Specimen collected from the Phillips coal bed in a road cut 4.8 miles northwest of Inman, Wise County, Virginia. 2. Modern film fern shown for comparison. 3. *Boweria schatzlarensis* (Stur) Kidston. Collected from a unclassified coal bed horizon located 3.1 miles South of Junction Routes 23 and 805, 1.1 miles South of Myra, Pike County, Kentucky.

PLATE II True Fern *Boweria*–1,1a. *Boweria schatzlarensis* (Stur) Kidston. Collected from a unclassified coal bed horizon located 3.1 miles South of Junction Routes 23 and 805, 1.1 miles South of Myra, Pike County, Kentucky.

Plate I True Ferns Boweria

Plate II True Ferns Boweria

PLATE I Seed Fern *Neuropteris*–1. *Neuropteris heterophylla* collected approximately 3 miles off State Route 83 on Route 604 just South of Vansant, Buchanan County, Virginia. 2, 2a. *Neuropteris Pocahontas*. Collected from the Pocahontas Number 2 coal bed horizon along Interstate Route 77 at a point 2.8 miles South of Flat Top, Mercer County, West Virginia.

PLATE II Seed Fern *Neuropteris*–1. *Neuropteris Pocahontas*. Collected from the Pocahontas Number 2 coal bed horizon along Interstate Route 77 at a point 2.8 miles South of Flat Top, Mercer County, West Virginia.

PLATE III Seed Fern *Neuropteris*–1, 1a. *Neuralethopteris jongmansii Laveine* collected from the mine roof in the Pocahontas No. 3 coal bed approximately 1200 feet below the Garden Creek hollow in Buchanan County, Virginia. 2. *Neuropteris ovata* (10X). Collected along Route 52 approximately 0.5 miles West of Maybuery, McDowell County, West Virginia (Note: there was no coal bed exposed).

PLATE IV Seed Fern *Neuropteris*–1. *Neuropteris scheuchzeri* 1a Enlarged view of a portion of 1 showing detail of the two small oval nearly rounded shaped pinnules at the base of the large pinuual where it attaches to the richis. The specimen was collected approximately 1 mile North of Stonega, Wise County, Virginia. Coal bed horizon unidentified. 2. *Osmunda regalis* also referred to as a Royal fern. Note the similarity between it and the fossil 1a.

PLATE V Seed Fern *Neuropteris*–1, 1a. *Neuropteris dussartii* collected from the Hazard #9 coal bed horizon 2.8 miles off Route 421 approximately 4 miles West of Hyden, Leslie County, Kentucky. 2,2a *Neuropteris obliqua*. Specimen collected at a strip mine where the Hazard #8(Francis)/#9 (Hidman) coal beds are mined in Aces Branch North off Lower Macintosh Road (KY-3425) 3.3 miles South East of Dryhill, Leslie County, Kentucky.

Plate I Seed Fern Neuropteris

Plate II Seed Fern Neuropteris

Plate III Seed Fern Neuropteris

Plate IV Seed Fern Neuropteris

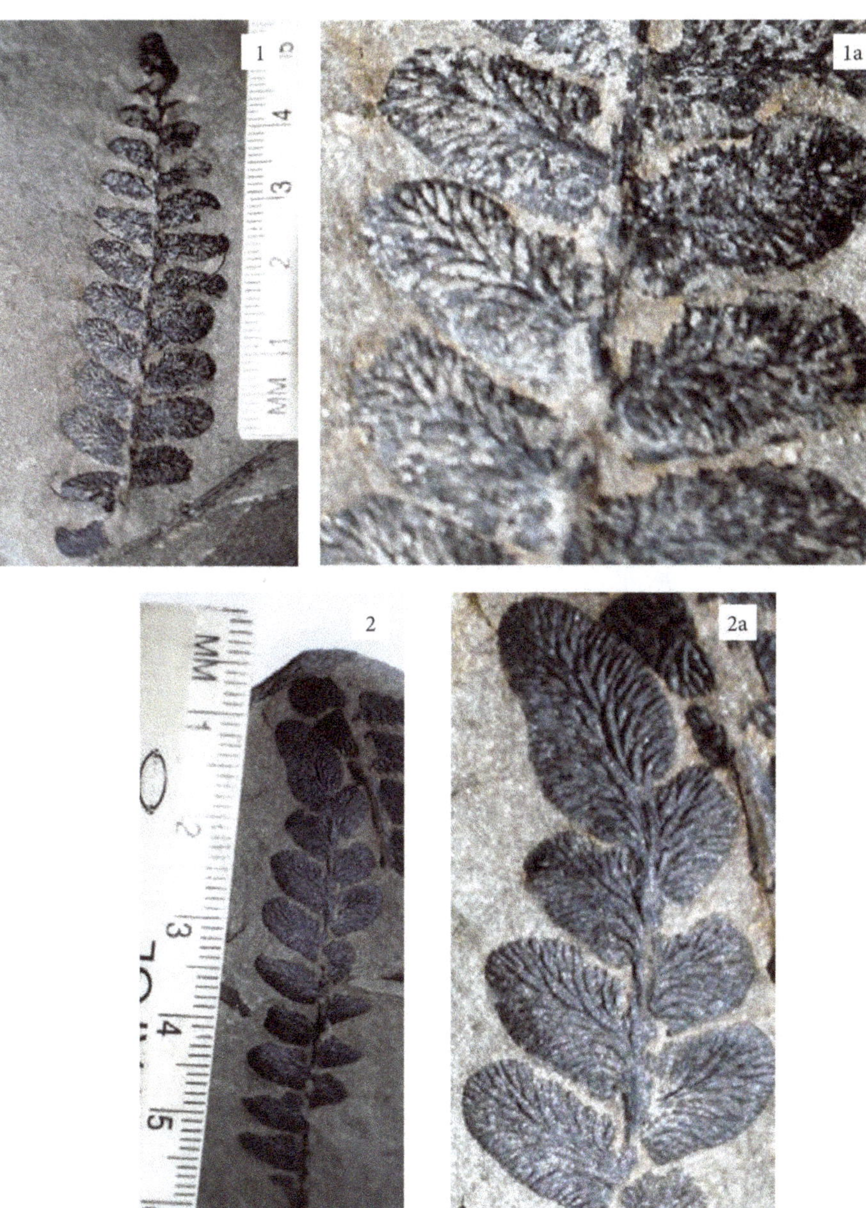

Plate V Seed Fern Neuropteris

Plate I–Seed Fern *Odontopteris*

1. *Odontopteris aequalis (osmundaformis).* Collected along Route 52 approximately 0.5 miles West of Maybuery, McDowell County, West Virginia (Note: there was no coal bed exposed).

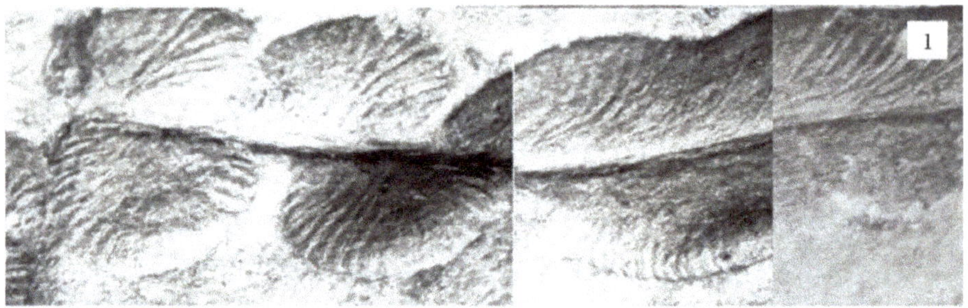

Plate I Seed Fern Odontopteris

Plate I–Seed Fern Seeds

1. Elongate form of *Trigonocarpus*. Collected from an unnamed coal bed. Road cut 0.2 miles North of Verna LN on State Route 23 southbound lane, approximately 6 miles from Jenkins, Letcher County, Kentucky. 2. *Trigonocarpus sp.* associated with a portion of a seed fern. Collected from the Taggart Marker coal bed 1.6 miles northwest off Route 78, 1 mile from Stonega, Wise County, Virginia.

Plate I: Seed Fern Seeds

Plate I–Seed Fern *Lyginopteris*

1. 1a, 1b *Lyginopteris cf. hoenighausi*. 1b is an enlargement of the stem showing thorn-like protrusions referred to as capitate glands (i.e. head-like shaped structure that secrets a fluid). Collected from the Powellton coal bed in a mine near Sharples, Logan County, West Virginia.

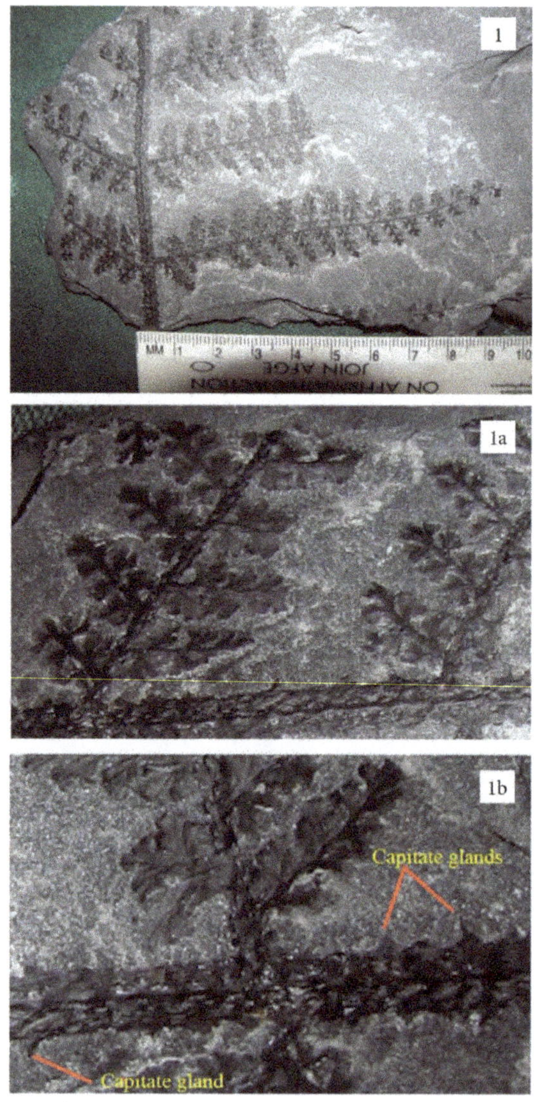

Plate I Seed Fern Lyginopteris

PLATE I–Seed Fern *Eusphenopteris*

1. 1a and 1b. *Euspenopteris nummularia*. Collected from a mine in the Lower Banner coal bed located at Red Onion Mountain approximately 10 miles East of Pound, Dickenson County, Virginia South of State Route 83.

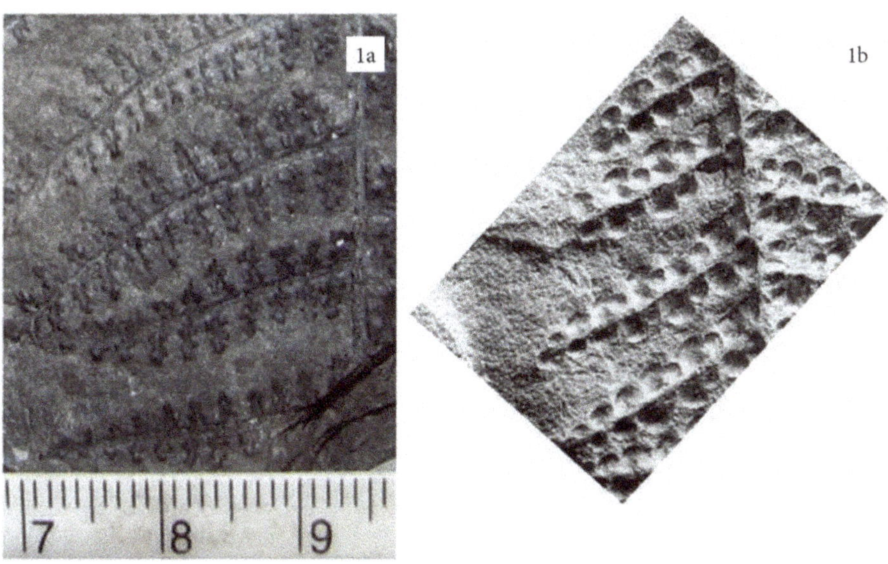

Plate V Seed Fern Neuropteris

CHAPTER 6

CORDAITES (EARLY GYMNOSPERMS)

CORDAITES were trees that reproduced from seeds and spores borne by cone-like structures considered by some to be an "early conifer" or gymnosperm (See Figure 37). They first appeared in the Upper Mississippian and then disappeared after the Triassic period. There are no extant descendants of Cordaites. Initially the name Cordaites was applied only to the narrow, strap-like compres-sion leaf remains, but it has come to be applied to the entire plant (See Figure 38). It is believed that one variety of the plant lived on dry land, while its shrub-like counterpart lived in marine-to-brackish water conditions on stilt-like root systems, much like the modern mangrove.

Figure 37: *Reconstruction of two varieties of Cordaites, one of which is a mangrove-type (left) and arboresent-type (right). Modified from Gillespie et. Al., 1978. Colorization by the author.*

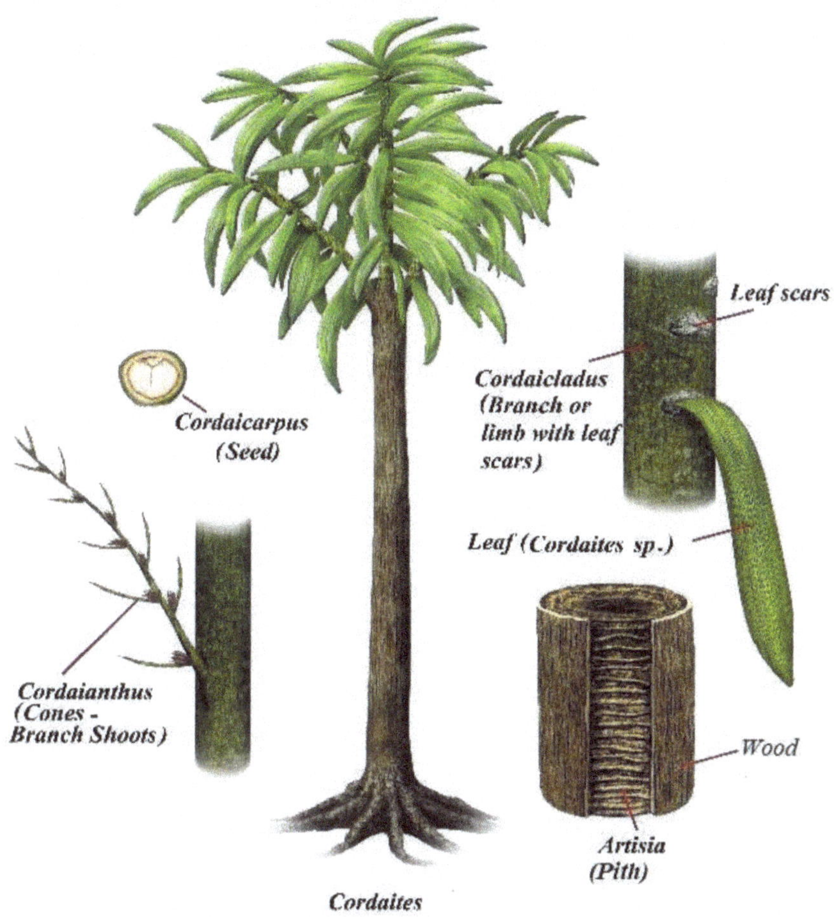

Figure 38: *Cordaites and its parts modified from Langford, G., 1958, figure 220, page 122 by permission of Esconi Associates, Illinois. Colorization courtesy of Jon Hughes/www.jfhdigital.com.*

PLATE I *Cordaites* –1,2 *Cordaties lingultus* (leaf). Coal horizon Imboden? Collected 1 mile North of Stonega, Wise County, Virginia. 3. Artisa sp. (stem). Collected above the Dorchester coal bed 2 miles North of the Junction Routes 624 and 83 near Georges Fork, Dickenson County, Virginia.

PLATE II *Cordaites–1, 1a Artisa sp*. (stem). All specimens collected from above a coal bed in road cut located 0.05 miles East of Junction Interstate 119 and Charlie White LN approximately 3 miles East of Milestone, Letcher County, Kentucky.

Plate I Cordaties

Plate II Cordaties

BIBLIOGRAPHY

Álvarez-*Vázquez*, C. and *Wagner*, RH. *2014*. Lycopsida from the lower Westphalian (Middle Pennsylvanian) of the Maritime *Provinces, Canada. Atlantic Geology, 50, pp. 167–232.*

Bashforth, Adren R, and Erwin L. Zodrow, 2007. "Partial reconstruction and paleoecology of Sphynophyllum costae (Middle Pennsylvanian, Nova Scotia, Canada)", Bulliten of Geosciences, vol., 82, issue 4, pp 365-382.

Cleal, Christopher, J. and Barry A. Thomas, 1994. "Plant fossils of the British coal measures", Paleontological Association, Field Guides to Fossils: Number 6, London, p.222.

Cross, A. T., Gillespie, W. H., and Taggart, R E., 1996. "Upper Paleozoic Vascular Plants," in *Fossils of Ohio*, edited by R M. Feldmann and Merrianne Hackathorn. Ohio Division of Geological Survey Bulletin 70, p. 396-479.

Department of Mines, Minerals and Energy, 2015, Coal Production in Virginia, Virginia Division of Geology and Mineral Resources https://www.dmme.virginia.gov/dgmr/coal.shtml.

DiMichele, William, A.,1980, Paralycopodites Morey & Morey, from the Carboniferous of Euramerica-a reassessment of generic affinities and evolution of "LEPIDODENDRON" Brevifolium Williamson, American Journal of Botany 67(10) pp 1466-1476.

DiMichele, William, A. Scott D. Elrick , and Richard M. Bateman, 2013, Grouth Habit of the Late Paleozoic Rhizomorphic tree-Ly-copsid Family Diaphorodendraceae: Phylogenetic,

Evolutionary, and Paleoecological Significance, American Journal of Botany 100(8) pp 1604–1625.

DiMichele, W.A. and Phillips, T.L. 1994. Paleobotanical and paleoecological constraints on models of peat formation in the Late Carboniferous of Euramerica, Palaeoclimatology, Palaeogeography, and Palaeoecology, 106:39-90

Gothan W. & Remy W., 1957. Steinkohlenpflanzen. Essen. Gillespie, William H., John A. Clendening, and Herman W. Pfefferkorn. 1978. "Plant Fossils of West Virginia." West Virginia Geological and Economic Survey, Education Series ED-3X: 172.

Hans Steur, 2017, Hans' Paleobotony Pages, Ellecom, The Netherlands

Jana Frojdová, Josef Pšenička , Jiří Bek , Christopher J. Cleal , 2017. Revision of the Pennsylvanian fern Boweria Kidston and the establishment of the new genus Kidstoniopteris. Review of Palaeobotany and Palynology236, Elsevier publishing, pp 33- 58.

Kenrick, Paul and Paul Davis, 2oo4, Fossil Plants, The Living Past Series, Smithsonian Books, Washington in association with the Natural History Museum, London, pp 216.

Langford, George, 1876. "The Wilington coal flora from a Pennsylvanian deposit in Will County, Illinois", republished by Esconi Associates appointed by the Earth Science Club of Northorn Illinois, 2 nd edition, 1958, p 366.

Lesquereux, Leo. "1879–1884: Description of the coal flora of the Carboniferous formation in Pennsylvania and through-out the United States." 2nd Pennsylvania Geological Survey Publication, 3 volumes.

Lewis, Richard, Q., Sr., 1978, Geologic map of the Hyden West quadrangle, Leslie and Perry Counties, Kentucky, GQ-1468.

McDowell, Robert, C., 2001, The geology of Kentucky—A text to accompany the Geologic Map of Kentucky, Chapter 7, Plate XXIV, USGS Professional Paper 1151-H.

McLoughlin,Thomas,F.,2017,Plant fossil atlas from(Pennsylvanian) carboniferous age found in central Appalachian coalfields, Top Link publishing, pp. 146.

Puffett, Willard, P., 1965, Geologic quadrangle map of Vicco quadrangle, GQ-418.

Seward, A.C., M.A., F.RS., 1898, Fossil Plants: A text-book for students of Botany and Geology, Cambridge University Press, London, Volume I, pp. 478

Seward, A.C., M.A., F.RS., 1898, Fossil Plants: A text-book for students of Botany and Geology, Cambridge University Press, London, Volume II, pp. 66

Seward, A.C., M.A., F.RS., 1898, Fossil Plants: A text-book for students of Botany and Geology, Cambridge University Press, London, Volume III, pp. 684

Steue, Hans. Hans' Paleobotony Pages, Ellecom, The Netherlands, May 10, 2017.

Wagner, Robert and Carmen-Álvarez-Vázquez, 2014, Atlantic Canada, Atlantic Geology, Vol. 50, pp167 - 232.

APPENDIX A

Floral Assemblages by collection site in Virginia

1. Wise Formation
    Pardee coal bed
    Located 6 miles West of Jct. of Rt. 68 and 160 West (N Inman St.), Appalachia, Wise County,Virginia.
    Coordinates: 82-15-55W 36-55-00N
    Fossils:
    1. *Lepidodendron sp.-Syringodendron*
    2. *Lepidodendron* in the stage of *Knorria*.
    3. *Lepidophloios*
    4. *Lepidodendron sporophyte* (small branch)
    5. *Lepidostrobophylum*
    6. *Lepidodendron* showing wood layers *Knorria* and *Aspidiopsis*.
    7. *Lepidophylloides*
    8. *Annularia spicata*
    9. *Bothrodendron sp.*

2. Wise Formation
    Phillips coal bed
    Located in a road cut 4.8 miles northwest of Inman, Wise County, Virginia.
    Fossils: 1. *Boweria sp.*

3.   Wise Formation
Taggart coal bed
Located 2.5 miles North of Stonega, Wise County, Virginia along State Route 600.
Coordinates: 82-47-17W 36-59-23N
Fossils:

    1. Lepidodendron The turbinatum
    2. Lepidodendron wortheni.
    3. Lepidophylloides (*Lepidendron* twig with leaves)
    4. Lepidodendron Knorria.
    5. Diaphorodendraceae
    6. Calamites suckowi.
    7. Calamites carinatus?
    8. Calamites sp.
    9. Calamophyllites
    10. Alloiopteris coalloides
    11. Sphenopteris souichii
    12. Mariopteris muricata.
    13. Mariopteris sphenopteroides.

4.   Wise Formation
Taggart coal bed horizon
Located 1.7 miles West off State Route 624 approximately 0.5 miles North of Junction Routes 624 and 606 near Keokee, Lee County, Virginia
Coordinates: 82-54-33W 36-52-14N
Fossils: 1. *Pecopteris plumose*

5.   Wise Formation
Taggart coal bed
Located approximately 1000 feet left off Route 160 3 miles northwest of the Junction Routes 160W and Route 68, Appalachia, Wise County, Virginia.
Coordinates: 82-51-14W 36-54-36N
Fossils: 1. *Mariopteris muricata*

6.   Wise Formation
Taggart Marker coal bed
Located 1.6 miles Northwest off Route 78 and 1 mile from Stonega, Wise County, Virginia.

Coordinates: 82-47-32W 36-58-39N
Fossils:
1. *Calamites sp.* preserved in pyrite
2. *Calamites ramifer* Stur, 1875
3. *Sphenopteris obtusiloba*
4. *Trigonocarpus sp.*
5. *Bergeria*

7. Wise Formation
Imboden coal bed
Located 1 mile North of Stonega, Wise County, Virginia along State Route 600.
Coordinates: 82-46-15W 36-57-57N
Fossils: 1. *Lepidodendron obovatum*

8. Wise Formation
Imboden coal bed
Located at Osaka, Wise County, Virginia.
Coordinates: 82-48-39W 36-56-49N
Fossils: 1. *Lepidodendron rigens*.

9. Wise Formation
Imboden coal bed
Located 1.3 miles North of Stonega, Wise County, Virginia.
Fossils: 1. *Calamites undulates*

10. Wise Formation
Imboden?
Collected 1 mile North of Stonega, Wise County, Virginia.
Fossils:
1. *Cordaties lingultus*
2. *Neuropteris scheuchzeri*

11. Wise Formation
Clintwood/Blair coal beds
Located 1 mile North of the Junction of State Route 83 and Camp Creek Road and 1 mile East of Georges Fork, Dickenson County, Virginia.
Coordinates: 82-30-41W 37-08-54N
Fossils: 1. *Pecopteris taiyuanensis*

12. Upper Norton Formation
     Dorchester coal bed
     Located 2 miles North of the Junction Route 624 and 83 near
     Georges Fork, Dickenson County, Virginia.
     Coordinates: 82-30-55W 37-09-00N
     Fossils:
     1. *Lepidostrobus* (reproductive cone).
     2. *Artisa approximata*
     3. *Artisa sp.*
     4. *Pinnularia (Myriophyllites)*

13. Upper Norton Formation
     Dorchester coal bed horizon
     Located 200 feet North of the Jct. of Roley Fleming Lane &
     Camp Creek Road 1 mile West of Georges Fork, Dickenson
     County, Virginia
     Coordinates: 82-31-17W 37-09-14N
     Fossils:
     1. *Sphenophyllum majus*
     2. *Sterophyllites*
     3. *Spenopteris sp*

14. Upper Norton Formation
     Norton coal bed
     Located 0.3 miles North of the Jct. of Rt. 623 and 624 Georges
     Fork, Dickenson County, Virginia.
     Fossils:
     1. *Calamites sp.*
     2. *Annularia radiate*
     3. *Pinnularia (Myriophyllites)*
     4. *Sphenopteris sp.*

15. Upper Norton Formation
     Splashdam coal bed
     Located 2.5 miles East of Haysi, Dickenson County, Virginia
     along Route 83 (Dickenson Highway) 0.4 miles from the
     Junction of Route 83 and 680.
     Coordinates: 82-12-41W 37-12-46N
     Fossils:
     1. *Calamites undulates*

> 2. *Calamites goeppertii.*
> 3. *Sphenopteris sp.*
> 4. *Sphenopteris obtusiloba,*

16. Upper Norton Formation
Lower Banner coal bed
Located at Red Onion Mountain approximately 10 miles East of Pound, Dickenson County, Virginia South of State Route 83.
Coordinates: 82-31-07W 37-06-38N
Fossils: 1. *Euspenopteris nummularia*

17. Upper Norton Formation
Kennedy coal bed
Located 1.5 miles South of Pilgroms Knob on State Route 680 on Saw Mill road, Buchanan County, Virginia.
Coordinates: 81-54-54W 36-54-36N
Fossils:
> 1. *Calamitina*
> 2. *Annularia radiata.*
> 3. *Annularia asteris.*
> 4. *Asterophyllities charaefomis*
> 5. *Sphenopteris crossotheca schatziarensis*
> 6. *Sphenopteris adiantoides*

18. Norton Formation
"unnamed" coal seam
Located along a railroad right of way parallel to the westbound lane along Route 58 inAppalachia, Wise County, Virginia.

19. Pocahontas Formation
Pocahontas No. 3 coal bed
Located in a shaft mine, approximately 1500 feet below the surface, near Keen Mountain, Buchanan County, Virginia.
Fossils:
> 1. *Calamities sp.*
> 2. *Neuralethopteris jongmansii Laveine*

20. Unclassified coal bed
    Located 3 miles off State Route 83 on Route 604 just North of Vansant, Buchanan County, Virginia.
    Fossils: 1. *Neuropteris heterophylla*

APPENDIX B

Floral Fontal Assemblages by collection site in Kentucky

1. Breathite Formation
    Hazard #9 coal bed horizon
    Located 2.8 miles off Route 421 approximately 4 miles West of Hyden, Leslie County, Kentucky.
    Coordinates: 83-23-52W 37-09-17N
    Fossils:
    1. *Cyclopteris sp.*
    2. *Cyclopteris orbicularis*
    3. *Sphenopteris sp.*
    4. *Neuropteris dussartii*

2. Breathite Formation
    Hazard #8(Francis)/#9 (Hidman) coal bed horizons
    Location Aces Branch North off Lower Macintosh Rd. (KY-3425) 3.3 miles South East of Dryhill, Leslie County, Kentucky.
    Coordinates: 83-20-20W 37-13-12N
    Fossils:
    1. *Lepidophyllum sp.*
    2. *Holonia tortuosa*
    3. *Lepidostrobus ovatifolius*
    4. *Calamites multiramus*
    5. *Calamites suckowi*

    6. *Asterophyllites equisetiformis* (Schlotheim) Brongniart
    7. *Annularia sphenophylloides.*
    8. *Calamostachys*
    9. *Sphenophyllym longifolium.*
    10. *Alethopteris valida*
    11. *Aphlebia arborescens*
    12. *Sphenopteris sp.*
    13. *Sphenopteris sewardii*
    14. *Eremopteris artimisiaefolia.*
    15. *Mariopteris acuta* Brongniart
    16. Karinopteris robusta
    17. *Neuropteris obliqua.*
    18. *Bothrodendron punctatum*

3.   Mingo formation
Upper Whitesburgh coal bed
Located in a road cut 0.3 miles East of Vicco, Perry County, Kentucky along I-15 at the Knott and Perry County boarder.
Coordinates: 83-01-46W 37-13-08N
Fossils:
    1. *Bothrodendron sp.*
    2. *Sphenopteris sp.*
    3. *Sphenopteris neuropteroides*

4.   Mingo formation
Williamson coal bed horizon
Located approximately 5 miles Southeast of Sideny, Pike County, Kentucky along U.S. Route 119.
Coordinates: 82-26-26W 37-34-05N
Fossils: 1. *Lepidostrobophyllum*

5.   Mingo formation
Kellioka coal bed
Coordinates: 83-00-38W 36-52-78N
Located near Homes Mill, Harlan County, Kentucky.
Fossils: 1. *Calamities suckowi*

6.   Mingo formation
     Amburgy coal bed
     Located 0.6 miles right off State Route 931 and 1.8 miles from
     the Junction of Route 931 and Route 15 North, Whitesburg,
     Letcher County, Kentucky.
     Coordinates: 82-49-17W 37-08-35N
     Fossils:
     1.   *Pecopteris parvula*
     2.   *Crenulopteris*

7.   Unclassified coal bed
     Located on Route 468 just North of Sidney, Pike County,
     Kentucky.
     Coordinates: 82-21-33W 37-37-15N
     Fossils: 1. *Palmatopteris furcate*

8.   Unclassified coal bed
     Located 0.05 miles East of Junction I-119 and Charlie White
     LN approximately 3 miles East of Millestone, Letcher County,
     Kentucky.
     Coordinates:82-44-05W 37-09-42N
     Fossils:
     1.   *Sphenopteris sp.*
     2.   *Mariopteris dernoncourti*

9.   Unclassified coal bed horizon
     Located 3.1 miles South of Junction Routes 23 and 805, 1.1
     miles South of Myra, Pike County, Kentucky.
     Coordinates: 82-35-58W 37-16-41N
     Fossils:
     1.   *Boweria schatzlarensis* (Stur) Kidston
     2.   *Annularia radiate*
     3.   Elongate form of *Trigonocarpus*

10. Unclassified coal bed
     Located at Vergie, Pike County, Kentucky.
     Coordinates: 82-34-39W 37-20-06N
     Fossils: 1. *Bothrodendron sp.*

11. Unclassified coal bed
    Located 0.5 miles North of Belfry, Pike County, KY along Route 119.
    Coordinates: 82-16-55W 37-37-40N
    Fossils: 1. *Calamostachys schimper*

APPENDIX C

Floral Fontal Assemblages by collection site in West Virginia

1. Pocahontas Formation
   Pocahontas #2 coal seam
   State Route 77 2.8 miles South of Flat Top, Mercer County, West Virginia.
   Fossils:
   > 1. *Lepidophloios protuberans*
   > 2. *Neuropteris Pocahontas*

2. Kanawha Formation
   Powellton coal bed
   Located in a mine near Sharples, Logan County, West Virginia.
   Fossils: 1. *Lyginopteris cf. hoenighausi*

3. No coal seam visible
   Located along Route 52 approximately 0.5 miles West of Maybuery, McDowell County, West Virginia.
   Fossils:
   > 1. *Neuropteris ovata*
   > 2. *Odontopteris aequalis (osmundaformis)*

This book is the second volume of a picture guide to Pennsylvanian (Carboniferous) age fossil plants and trees found in the central Appalachian coalfields which include southwest Virginia, southeast Kentucky and southwest West Virginia. This book complements and is a continuation of a previously published book on the same subject in 2017.

ABOUT THE AUTHOR

A Bachelor of Science degree was earned while attending Morehead State University at Morehead, Kentucky. In December of 1979 I completed my Master Thesis in geology at Eastern Kentucky University in Richmond, Kentucky. Then in June 1980 I joined the U.S. Department of Labor Mine Safety and Health Administration (MSHA). I stayed with this agency as a geologist and coal mine inspector for 28 years collecting plant fossils in the coal mines and outcrops (road cuts) in south-western Virginia. For approximately 26 years I taught introduction to geology courses at colleges in Cumberland, Kentucky and Wise, Virginia. I started out in geology as a "rock hound" collecting rocks, minerals and fossils. By the end of high school I decided to become a geologist and attended college. Actually my parents insisted that I leave home because it was overtaken by my rock samples. During high school and college I practiced lapidary work making jewelry from minerals and rocks.